Go and Get It

Making Happiness Permanent in Your Life

Yadwiga Fazzina

Book Publishers Network
P.O. Box 2256
Bothell • WA • 98041
Ph • 425-483-3040
www.bookpublishersnetwork.com

10 9 8 7 6 5 4 3 2 1

Printed in the United States of America

LCCN   2012950404
ISBN   978-1-937454-59-3

Editor: Julie Scandora
Cover Designer: Laura Zugzda
Typographer: Stephanie Martindale

Now when I passed by thee, and looked upon thee, behold, thy time was the time of love; and I spread my skirt over thee, and covered thy nakedness: yea, I sware unto thee, and entered into a covenant with thee, saith the Lord GOD, and thou becamest mine.

Then washed I thee with water; yea, I throughly washed away thy blood from thee, and I anointed thee with oil.

I clothed thee also with broidered work, and shod thee with badgers' skin, and I girded thee about with fine linen, and I covered thee with silk.

I decked thee also with ornaments, and I put bracelets upon thy hands, and a chain on thy neck.

And I put a jewel on thy forehead, and earrings in thine ears, and a beautiful crown upon thine head.

Thus wast thou decked with gold and silver; and thy raiment was of fine linen, and silk, and broidered work; thou didst eat fine flour, and honey, and oil: and thou wast exceeding beautiful, and thou didst prosper into a kingdom.

And thy renown went forth among the heathen for thy beauty: for it was perfect through my comeliness, which I had put upon thee, saith the Lord GOD.

Ezekiel 16:8-14 (King James Version)

Contents

Introduction

On January 5, I awoke at three o'clock in the morning with all kinds of strange and wondrous thoughts coming into my head. The thoughts flowed with urgency, like a torrent that I could not stop whether I wanted to or not. So I put on the light and began to write them down, line after line, writing densely on a single-spaced tablet, front and back. I wrote furiously, non-stop, for twelve straight hours. When my hand became cramped and numb, I started talking into a tape recorder. I recorded eight tapes all together, and when I was all done—about eighteen hours later—I was breathless, stunned, amazed about the experience I had just had. I had felt compelled to write and speak for hours on end, from a voice that was coming not from me, but through me. The result is the very book that you are reading.

Chapter 1

The Question Everybody Asks

Hello. Congratulations for picking up this book. Now you are about to discover something that you've never heard about before, something you've never imagined, something that has never entered your mind. If you read through this book, you will discover something that you didn't think existed in this life. And when you find it out, you will wonder how it has happened that you have lived so many years without knowing about it.

I am talking about a new way of living, a new way of looking at life, and this new way will blow your mind away. You may ask—*Why do you think you know what this life is all about? And who made you an expert?* Well, I am just like you but with a tiny little difference. I know because I tried, I searched, I did not stop, and I did not give up. I put away everything in my life to find the answer to the question everyone on earth is asking—*Why am I here?*

I don't care who you are, what you do, how old you are, or what you think about yourself; I know you are interested in this question because you have picked up this book. As long as you are holding this book in your hand, please keep reading. This book will change your life, and I guarantee it.

Over the years, I've asked myself questions—*What is my purpose in life? What is my passion? Why am I always searching and trying? Why I am always unsatisfied, no matter what I do, what I say, how I look?*

By the time I was thirty years old, I had accomplished everything I had dreamed about. I had a good job with a major aerospace company, a sports car, and a nicely decorated condominium. I had more money than I ever needed, and I was young and beautiful. But I was miserable. The only thing I wanted was to be happy. My search for happiness took a long time, and finally now, at last, I have found out the source of my unhappiness. In the process of looking for an answer, I wasted lots of time that I could have spent enjoying my life. I'd like to share my experience with you so you can avoid my mistakes.

I've found that my happiness has nothing to do with my age, my job, how much money I have, who loves me, or how beautiful I am. You see, today, I am middle-aged, and I am all alone. You ask—*How can you be happy when you are middle-aged and all alone?* But I am happy and that is what this book is all about. It is not about me and my life, but about my discovery of a new way of living.

What would you do if, out of the blue, a stranger came to you and told you that you have a chance for a new beginning? What if, during the first part of your life, you lived in a cocoon, dark and restricted, and suddenly you had a chance to outgrow it and live as freely as a butterfly? Would you be interested? Would you try? Would you take a chance?

You do have that chance to start your life all over again. This new chance I am talking about is even better because if you were to start all over again the way that you are right now, chances are that you will make the same or similar mistakes as before. With this new chance, you will be seeing your life in a new perspective, and at the same time, you will be making new decisions and better ones than before. Think about this: You will be a new person with a new character and a new way of looking at life, yourself, and other people. You will be no longer like a gray caterpillar, crawling in the dust; you will be like a beautiful colorful butterfly, rising up higher and higher, seeing things you have never seen before.

You are going to start your new life as a transformed person.

The Treasure

In this life, there is something hidden from the human eye. Just as with treasure hidden deep down in the earth, the only way you can find it is to dig down and search for it. When you find this treasure, it will be so priceless to you that you will guard it, watch it, and take care of it so no one will be able to steal it away from you. This hidden treasure I am talking about is so priceless and so wonderful that you will sell everything you have to get it. You will search for it, and when you find it, you will wonder at how poor and empty your life was before and how it was possible for you to live that way. And when you have found it, you will keep it—and treasure it—to the end of your life.

This treasure is available to everybody. But first, you have to need it with all your heart, and you have to want it as much as a person dying of thirst wants water. If you've never wanted anything as badly as this in your life, maybe it's because you never thought that what I am talking about was possible to discover and to possess.

Maybe you're asking yourself: *Okay. So, how should I start? Where should I look? What should I do first?* First of all, when you start reading this book, you have to start thinking in a new way; you have to be willing to open up your mind. You have to stretch your imagination and understanding. You have to think like a little child hearing a fairy tale. You have to be willing to look far behind what you learned so far about life. You have to stop thinking the old way, about your past failures and the bad things that have happened in your life before, and you have to open yourself up to new magical possibilities.

To understand this book, you have to start all over again with a clean, clear mind, as if you know nothing about life. As you are reading, put away your judgments and opinions, and slowly, when you begin to see the whole picture, you will understand. You will see the truth, and the truth will set you free.

I used to say—*I wish I could be just like a bird and run away from this mad, cruel, unfair life, full of pain and sadness.* People told me in reply—*You can't just run away. You will be part of this world until you die, and before you die, you will be full of bitterness and regret. You will feel as if you've lost your life because you'll have made lots of mistakes and not done the things you wanted to do. You had a chance for a good life, but you messed it up, and now it is too late.*

I listened to them, but I did not believe. I was stubborn, and I was determined to prove to them that they were wrong and I was right. Well, I've succeeded.

Second Chance

I tell you because it's true. Your life does not have to be this way; you can have a second chance. You can be happy, no matter where you are in your life right now. You can turn it around and be a winner. All you have to do is make a choice. You can choose to live a different, happy life, or you can choose to do nothing about your unhappy life. You can choose to feel joy and peace rather than bitterness, regret, and loss. And one day on your deathbed, surrounded by your family and those who love you, you will be able to say: *I lived a happy and fruitful life, and now I am ready to go to my Maker.*

First, to make a change, you have to understand one very simple thing. Life is not what you see. Look back to your origins. You were born into this world a perfect little baby. There was no pollution in your mind, no pain, no fear, no anger, no shame. You came into this world and into your parents' arms an innocent, and at that moment, all the madness in your life began.

Perhaps you saw your parents fighting and screaming. Perhaps they even screamed at you or expected you to be something you were not made to be. Maybe you went to school and could not concentrate because you remembered your mother calling you stupid. Perhaps your teachers told you that you were a bad student and would not amount to anything. Maybe your father abused you physically and mentally. Maybe you grew up, went to work, and then got fired for making a mistake. Or maybe you couldn't even find work because your father never worked and you didn't know where to begin. Maybe your mother took drugs and alcohol during her pregnancy, and now you struggle with the same addictions. Perhaps you had a pretty normal, benign upbringing but eventually grew up to a world full of compromise and lies, war and terrorism, crime and murder, destructive weaponry, corrupt politicians, and cruel leaders. After living for a while, you realize that you are living in a mad, mad, mad world—a world that you did nothing to create, a world you were simply born into, a world you feel helpless to change.

Before you know it, you feel confused, lost, and full of fears. You don't know what to do or how to disconnect from your bad upbringing or this hostile, fearful world. Who is to blame, after all? Your parents, your teachers, your boss, your president? So perhaps you say to yourself—*I have to fight to stay alive. I have to protect myself, I have to get what I can out of this life, no matter the cost.*

And maybe that's exactly what you did. You protected yourself and got what you could, no matter the cost. But before you knew it, you became just like "them"—the people who disillusioned you. And that is where you are right now—just like them. Maybe you say—*No way, I am not just like them. I am a good person. I give and give, but everybody is after me. Everyone is trying to use me, take advantage of me. They call me names behind my back and want to destroy me.*

Let me ask you a question. *Why do you think that you are any different than "they" are?* People are like monkeys. We live together; we learn from each other and imitate each other. We are so lost that we don't know what is right and what is wrong anymore. But you don't have to be this way. You face two choices: You can stay bitter and angry, blaming the world for what has happened to your life; or you can disconnect yourself, you can cut yourself loose, and you can remove the feeling of discontent and unhappiness that the past has brought on you.

So you ask—*What should I do then?* There is only one answer to this question—you have to learn a new way to live in this world. You have to change by renewing yourself. By learning who you really are. What you are here for. Where you come from and where you are going. You have to find out the truth about yourself.

Two Kingdoms

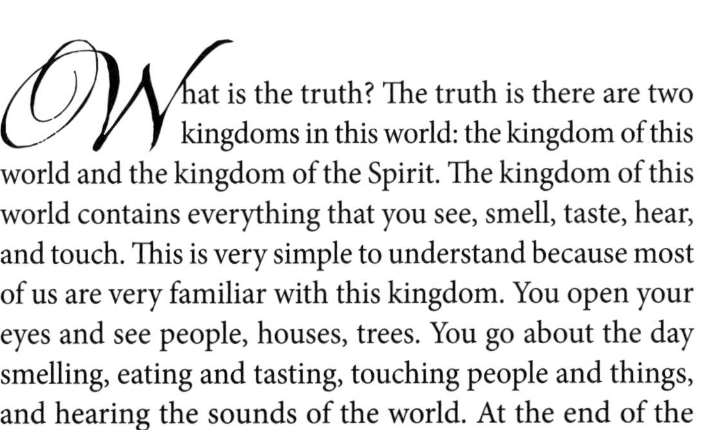

What is the truth? The truth is there are two kingdoms in this world: the kingdom of this world and the kingdom of the Spirit. The kingdom of this world contains everything that you see, smell, taste, hear, and touch. This is very simple to understand because most of us are very familiar with this kingdom. You open your eyes and see people, houses, trees. You go about the day smelling, eating and tasting, touching people and things, and hearing the sounds of the world. At the end of the day, you sleep. And you think that this is your whole life.

But this is only one tiny little part of your life. There is another, bigger part to your life—that of your spirit. When you open up your eyes, your spirit looks through the windows of your eyes and sees something entirely different.

Besides the kingdom of our physical world, there is a spiritual world, a powerful kingdom of its own. It may be hard to accept, but the spirit is more real than your body. If all of your senses are shut down, your spirit lives on. When your body sleeps, your spirit lives on. When you are in a coma, your spirit lives on. When you are anesthetized during an operation, your spirit lives on. And when you die, your spirit lives on.

Perhaps you are so used to living in your body that you don't even know that your spirit exists. But the spirit is your life, and without the spirit, you are dead. Oh yes, you live on in the physical kingdom, but what kind of life is it? I tell you, if you could only get in touch with your spirit, you would find out that right here inside you are all the answers to your questions, problems, and unhappiness.

Kingdom of This World

Now let me tell you about the kingdom of this world. You say—*Why are you calling it a kingdom? Doesn't a kingdom have to have a king?*

Yes, this kingdom does have a king. But first, we need to talk about the king's subjects. When you were struggling with some unwanted behavior, have you ever told yourself that you wouldn't do it anymore but kept on doing it anyway? For instance, you promised yourself that you wouldn't yell at your wife anymore or hit your son or drink or eat too much. But no matter how many times you promised yourself, you continued to do it over and over again. You ask yourself—*Why do I do these things that I don't want to do? There is something inside of me that makes me do it.*

Yes, there is something inside of you that makes you do it—and it is called evil. Evil makes you do it. Then, who is in control of you? Evil is in control, and because it is in control of you and everything in this world, evil is the king of this world. You ask—*Are you telling me that there is no good in me?* Of course there is good in you, but evil controls the good. You see, evil whispers into your ear and tries to deceive you, lie to you, manipulate you, and tempt you to do exactly the things you don't want to do.

Even if you want to do "good," you won't see anything good come from it when evil is in control. For instance, let's say that you lend money to somebody in need. Time goes by, and you find yourself thinking (the evil)—*He didn't even say "Thank you." Is he going to give me the money back? I saw him buying lots of things today. What happens if I don't have enough money for my rent?* You find yourself thinking that you are sorry for lending money to this person, for doing this good thing.

Are you about to say—*What crap! Am I that stupid? Why am I reading this book? Why should I believe that evil is whispering in my ear?* But wait. Please remember to keep your mind open and try to think a new way. History has many examples of times when people were called upon to think in a new way, and I am asking you do to the same. Remember that a flat world certainly made sense to people at one time, but the truth of a round world prevailed. So please keep reading, and when you see the big picture, you will understand.

So let's continue. You say—*Are you telling me that something is standing next to me and whispering in my ear to think evil thoughts or do bad deeds?* Yes, if you really pay attention, you will acknowledge that you know this voice. I don't know where these evil thoughts come from, but I do know that they are there. When you hear these thoughts, you might listen to them, and then you might act on them. You have a choice whether to act on them or not. But everything that you do, you do because you first entertained the thought.

People ask—*Why is there so much pain and suffering in this world?* There is so much pain and suffering in this world because sometime, somehow, somewhere, someone listened to his evil thought and made a wrong decision. You ask—*Then, how can we fight evil thoughts? How can we stop thinking? How can we discern which thoughts are evil thoughts and which thoughts are good thoughts?*

You are not going to be able to stop bad thoughts coming to your mind, no matter how much you try, until you understand the other kingdom.

Kingdom of Spirit

This kingdom of the Spirit is not like the kingdom of this world. You can see, smell, touch, hear, and feel the kingdom of the Spirit but only with the senses of your spirit. Right now, all those senses in your spirit remain dull until you make a choice to receive them, to make them sharp.

To understand this, I need to tell you a story. Please keep your mind open and try not to form an opinion of this story until you see the whole picture. This is the most important story you will ever hear because it will help you to understand your whole life: your way of thinking, your way of doing things, your pains, your joys, and your future.

Spirits

A long, long time ago, there was no earth, and there was no light. There was only Spirit hovering over the emptiness. The Spirit was without smell and without touch and was called God. The Spirit always was and always will be; there was (and is) no beginning or end to the Spirit.

The Spirit was not alone. There were other spirits keeping God company. These spirits were called angels, and they were different from God. Angels were not able to love and did not have the power to create or to destroy. The angels had other roles to play, as they were servants of God and did what God told them to do. Some were singers and some worshipers. God had power over all, including the angels, who existed to help God.

God and the angels lived in the happy, beautiful place called heaven. God kept everything in order and under control. In heaven, everything had a purpose, everything existed for a reason. And peace reigned.

Lucifer was most the beautiful angel of them all. His responsibility was to play music, and he made beautiful music indeed. One day, Lucifer decided that he did not want to be an angel anymore; he wanted to be just like God. Lucifer talked with other angels and convinced some of them of his point of view. One third of the angels left heaven and began to plot against God. This is how evil become real. There was knowledge of good and evil before, but evil had not yet been made manifest—not until Lucifer.

One day, God began thinking about making a creature in His image, someone to love and to share with, someone to love Him in return, someone better than the angels. Because God is love, He wanted someone to love. And God wanted to have a family that would understand Him, talk to Him, and walk with Him. This new creature would have freedom and choice; he would come to God by his own will and could choose whether to love Him.

God needed to put His new creation in a physical place. So God created this place just by saying a word—and He called it earth. Earth was meant to be a temporary place for His creation. When everything was created that needed creating, God looked and saw that everything was very good.

Then God come down to the earth and formed a body from sand and water. He knelt down next to the body and breathed His own Spirit into the nostrils. And a human being was created. God's Spirit, His very essence, was breathed into the human body. And this body thus became a temporary home for God's Spirit.

God named this new creature Adam. Now Adam was made just like God but had a body. Adam's love for God would not be free if God forced his will on Adam. So God made him a free human being. He had his own free will and was able to make choices.

God placed Adam on the earth in the place called Eden. Eden was a beautiful place with gardens, rivers, trees, and plenty of fruits. Adam had everything that he needed and wanted. God walked and talked with Adam in the coolness of the day. God and Adam were family to each other, and they loved one another. Then one day, God looked at Adam and decided that Adam should not be alone. God put Adam to sleep, removed one rib from Adam's side, and from this rib, formed a woman. God brought the woman to Adam, and the woman became his wife. Adam called her Eve.

Now, God looked, and He saw that everything was perfect. God's plan was done. God said to Adam and Eve, "You are free to eat from any tree in the garden, but you must not eat from the Tree of Good and Evil for when you eat of it you will surely die."

You must understand why death comes from eating the fruit from the Tree of Good and Evil. God is only pure and clean, and His Spirit cannot live in the presence of evil. God is the purifier so everything impure will be destroyed. Knowing about evil is one thing. But when you choose evil, you become separate from God's Spirit.

One day as Eve was walking around the Tree of Good and Evil, Lucifer crept into the Garden of Eden disguised as a snake. He coiled around the Tree of Good and Evil and whispered into Eve's ear that she should eat the fruit from that tree. He lied to Eve and tempted her, saying that if she ate the fruit, she would not die but would become just like God. So Eve ate the fruit and gave some to Adam.

After God had breathed His Spirit into Adam, Adam was no longer a lump of clay and dirt. He became a life made in the image of God. God is life. God is also love and purity.

When Eve and Adam ate the fruit, they lost God's purity. When they ate evil, they were poisoned. They became what they ate. Adam's spirit was death now. He was deceived; he didn't know what he was doing. He had never encountered evil before; he had never known anything but perfection, purity, cleanliness, freedom.

Can you imagine Adam in the beginning? Newly created by God, pure and perfect, walking without fear, without pain, without anything that creates destruction. Then Eve came into the garden, perfect, pure, and beautiful as well. Imagine how much they loved each other right away and how there were no limits, no walls, no inhibitions between them. Can you imagine a love without evil? A love where everything is said and done from the heart, with no jealousy, no manipulation, no attempt to have power or control over the other? That is the love that Adam and Eve had in Eden.

But as soon as they ate the fruit of the Tree of Good and Evil, they lost the Spirit of God. They became death to the spirit, and they became evil. For the first time in their lives, they realized what evil was.

Everything changed for them from that moment on. They knew something was wrong because they began to experience new and unusual things. There was darkness. They realized they were naked because the glory of God was not covering them anymore. Fear come over them and paralyzed them. Can you imagine how they felt? In a single moment, love became hate, honesty became a lie, beauty became ugliness, health became sickness. In the twinkle of an eye, they had been changed. They became frightened and started to run away.

When God saw what had happened, he called Adam, but Adam hid and did not answer. When God asked Adam why he was hiding, he lied. And once again, he felt shame.

Now Adam and Eve had to leave, to go away from Eden. They could no longer stay in this pure and beautiful place. As they fled, darkness, cold, and thunder surrounded them. I have a sense that there was no physical thunder, rain, or darkness but that they experienced these things as a vision of evil and of their own fear.

After the sin, God still loved Adam and Eve. Everything that He had created for them was still theirs, the inheritance from father to children. In spite of God's love, they had to leave Eden. They left feeling sorry, ashamed, full of regret, and fearful of the future that was ahead of them. Now they had to begin providing for themselves: working hard for food and shelter and earning their way with pain, labor, and the sweat of their brows. As they left paradise, their faces and spirits hung close to the ground—and they felt the utter shame of sin and defeat.

God's Plan for Redemption

What a devastating story, what a devastating vision for God to contemplate. What a defeat for God. At the same moment, as God watched Adam and Eve's departure, He was thinking: I love them so much that I'm going to fight for them and take them back. I will make a plan so they will be able to come back to me, and we will be the same as we were before. I know that we will be together again.

God knew that Adam and Eve were in Lucifer's trap now and under his control. They became cursed, and the ground they worked became cursed. From that time on, every person born of Adam and Eve was cursed.

To understand this, we have to return to the tree and its fruits. When a tree becomes poisoned, the healthy fruit growing on it also becomes poisoned. And this poison had become an integral part of Adam and Eve. So, no matter how much Adam and Eve tried, they were now controlled and ruled by evil. The penalty for every sin became death. Now every person after Adam and Eve was condemned to die. Their spirits would follow after Satan in death, to live with him and be united with him.

God knew there was only one way to break this cycle of sin in His creation: A new person must come willingly into the world to take the curse from it. That person would have to come from somewhere other than this world and not be born of Adam and Eve. It would have to be someone with God's Spirit in him, someone clean and pure. The people of earth could not perform this sacrifice, not because they did not want to do it but because they no longer had the Spirit of God in them.

God said, "I want my children back; I cannot leave them lost and alone. The only way that I can do this is to go to earth as a human being. I will live with my children. I will tell them who God is and how much God loves them."

Now, there is one God, but He is expressed in three ways: Father, Word (Son), and Spirit. Word is everything that God says. Before God created light, He formed a picture in his mind about how light should look, and then He said, "Let there be light," and there was light. The word "light" became materialized exactly how God saw it in His mind. So God can create anything from nothing, just by saying the word. Human beings, in contrast, can only create from something already created.

So, first there was a Word. God was going to send the Word to the earth so the Word would have to become materialized. The way He would become materialized was for the Word to become a seed. That seed would be born on the earth and become human. In this way, He would become both Son of God and human too.

God knew that if He came to this earth, Satan would try to use the same dirty tricks on Him that he had used on God's people. He knew that Satan would lie, cheat, steal, and manipulate, but Satan's tricks would not work on God because He would have His Spirit within Him. He would be able to resist every evil temptation from Satan and live on earth without sin.

God said, "Before I go to earth, I have to be born into the family. Everyone on this earth is My child, but I want My Son to be born to a new family, a new tribe." So God chose a righteous man named Abraham who was walking perfectly with Him. God told Abraham his plan that He would make Abraham father of a nation. He told Abraham that every child born to him would be a part of a great new nation and that kings would be born of this nation. And so it came to be.

Many generations after Abraham, a girl named Mary from the tribe of Abraham was born. When she was fourteen or fifteen years old, she was betrothed to a man named Joseph. God sent the angel Gabriel to earth to speak to Mary, and the angel said, "Fear not, Mary. You have found favor with God. You shall conceive a son in your womb, and you shall call him Jesus. He shall be great and called the Son of the Highest. The Lord God shall give Him a throne, and there shall be no end to his kingdom. He is going to save people from sin and destruction. Because of Him, people will be able to come back to God."

Mary was surprised that the God of her father, the God that she had prayed to for so many years, the God she heard about all her life, now was going to be a child in her womb. She said, "How is this possible? I have never been with a man before."

Gabriel explained to her that the Holy Spirit would come upon her, and the power of the Highest would over-shadow her. And the holy being that would be born of her would be called the Son of God. Mary did not understand, but she knew that if God said it, it would happen as He said. And this is exactly what happened. Mary became pregnant and gave birth to a son in a Bethlehem manger. And she called her son Jesus.

Just think. The little baby lying in Mary's arms—so tiny, so vulnerable—was God. The all-powerful, all-knowing God was born on this earth to give Himself to us—to people. To people who would reject Him. To people full of evil and anger who would humiliate and kill Him. For this, He had left the kingdom of peace, love, and beauty and come to the dark and miserable kingdom of earth.

Jesus was going to experience pain, misery, and death in this evil kingdom just as His creation was experiencing it simply because, long ago, they did not listen to Him and they did not believe Him. But God was looking over the little baby Jesus and protecting Him. Jesus had to survive in this world because God had a big plan for Him.

Jesus was going to accomplish what He was sent to earth to do. He came to this earth and to His creation, and they did not even recognize Him, they did not know Him, and they did not want Him. But Jesus loved His people. He was not going to give up on them. Jesus knew that they didn't know any better; they only knew this world and the evil in it.

So Jesus taught people about the kingdom of God. He told them what it is like to live in the Kingdom of God, to belong to it. He told them what it is like to be free from fear, pain, and sickness. His teachings were new to them; they had never heard of this new way of living and were not able to comprehend it. Their minds were so focused on this world and their usual way of living that they could not accept the new way. Jesus performed miracles to prove that if He was able to do impossible things, then He was certainly able to make them free and healthy and happy. They still did not believe Him. So Jesus walked on this earth to spread the news of the Kingdom of God. And then He was to die.

Why Did He Have to Die?

The penalty of sin is death. When we sin, we are going to die. If we continue to live on this earth the way that we do now, we will die. If we continue to live in sin, we will vegetate and be miserable. And when we die, not only will our body die but also our spirit will go to be with Satan and live with him in pain. If you think that it's horrible to live on earth now with Satan trying to own you, can you imagine how it's going to be when Satan has you in his clutches forever? Because the penalty for sin is death. The only way you will not die is to stop sinning. But you already know that if you remain in your current situation you will not be able to stop sinning.

What would you think if someone came and willingly died for your sins, if someone took away your sins and made you pure and clean as if you had never sinned before? You would not sin. You would only do the things that you really want to do. You would not think about doing things that give you pain, shame, and confusion. You would be clean, pure, healthy, and happy. And death would have no power over you.

So someone had to die for our sins. That is why Jesus came to this earth, to die for your sins, to take away your sins, and to make you free.

How was this going to be accomplished? Jesus was going to die for the very people that He had created. They were going to kill Him. Because Jesus was on this earth and living in the kingdom where sin had dominion over people, He died just like every other person on this earth. He went to hell like every person on this earth as well, but Jesus was not held in hell because He did not sin. Hell could not hold a pure, clean person. So, although Jesus died as a human being, He was resurrected as a perfectly pure and clean person, with God's Spirit in Him.

Satan was thinking, *This is the Son of God, and when I kill Him, I will finally be like God.* Satan continued to want God's power, just as in the beginning. But Satan did not know that by killing Jesus he was doing God a favor. Satan does not know God's law, and that is why he can never win with God. And that is why Satan can create havoc in this life but he can never finally win.

Jesus took all of our past and future sins on His shoulders. And when He died, He went to hell and left our sins there. Jesus carried the sins of all creation on His shoulders, and after three days in hell, he rose up. Satan thought that he had won, but Jesus was resurrected.

After the resurrection, Jesus showed Himself to the apostles and His followers before He was taken up to Heaven. He told His followers, "Wait for the promise of the Father that you have heard about from Me. For John truly baptized with water, but you shall be baptized with the Holy Spirit and receive the power of the Holy Spirit upon you."

When He had spoken these things, He was taken up.

After Jesus had gone, the apostles did not know what had happened, and they did not know what to do. After Jesus's death, the Christians were afraid and went into hiding. They gathered to pray in secret. Jesus's death was a tragedy for them. The apostles had walked with Him and listened to Him. Everything that He had said to them was simply out of this world, out of their experience. His teachings were so different and so new that they could not comprehend them; they could not understand. They wondered: How are the things that Jesus taught us going to happen? How was this new way of being going to work?

Forty days later, one hundred twenty of Jesus's followers were gathered in the Upper Room to pray. Suddenly, there came a sound from heaven, as of a rushing mighty wind, and it filled the entire household. And there appeared unto them cloven tongues like fire, and the fiery tongues rested upon each of them. At that moment, they were all filled with the Holy Spirit and began to speak in other tongues, as the Spirit had given them utterance.

The same Spirit that God had breathed into Adam's nostrils was now put into them. They became God's children again. They returned to the fold, His family. They had walked with Jesus, and now, even if they were about to face persecution, they had chosen God. God promised them what He had promised Jesus: resurrection and new life. God's Spirit was in them now, and they were God's children. They belonged to Him, and Satan no longer had any claim to them.

At the same moment, they started speaking in other tongues. What did this mean? The Spirit of God was expressing Himself in them, and they were full of joy and exuberance. The Spirit of God had come to his disciples and was living in them. They had become like Adam and Eve before they sinned; they were once again the beloved children of God.

Salvation

So what really happened when Jesus was resurrected? Jesus opened the door for us to go back to God and to be with Him as Adam and Eve were before they sinned. The difference is that now we know about good and evil and Adam did not know. The difference is that now we can choose whether to be children of God or children of Satan. There is nothing in between: We cannot stand in the middle between God and Satan. Now, there is a choice. Now, either we live in the kingdom of this world, or we live in the Kingdom of God.

Adam didn't know the difference, but we do, and because we do, we are not in the same danger of falling, of sinning, of dying. Instead, we can make the choice to be with God.

You may ask—*How do we do make this choice?* It's very simple. As simple as asking God to forgive you for your sins and to take you back as His child. You ask—*Why do I need to do that?* You need to ask God to forgive you for your sins because it is the only way you can be free.

Let's say your friend says something hurtful to you and you are angry. Your friend replies, "I didn't realize I would make you angry because I said the same thing to someone else and he didn't get angry." Then your friend walks away without apologizing. Are you going to forget this incident? No, you will not forget this incident, and furthermore, you will stay away from your friend. On the other hand, if your friend had apologized and asked for your forgiveness, your relationship would have taken on a whole new dimension.

It is the same situation with God. Maybe you are not aware that you are sinning, and maybe as the result of Adam and Eve, you are not to blame for your sins. But if you do not ask God for forgiveness, you will not be cleansed.

The only way to come back to God is to ask Him because you, alone, have the choice. God is a gentleman and will not force Himself upon you. By creating you in His likeness, He has given you free will. God said, "I've put open doors in front of you: one to good and blessing and one to evil and destruction. I've made it possible for you to come back to me. Make a choice."

Because this is the key. When you seek the kingdom of God first, everything else will be added to you. Let's say a man proposes to a woman and she agrees to be his wife. She does not have to ask him if her young daughter can come and live with them. The woman knows without question that, wherever she goes and whatever she receives, her daughter goes with her and will receive the same.

It's the same way with God. If you accept God as your father, everything that He has is yours—all the gifts, all the goodies, all the blessings. On the other hand, when you accept God as your father, He takes everything to Himself that is yours—your problems, sorrows, pain, sickness, fears, and mistakes. You might ask—*We receive all His blessings, and He takes all our miseries?* Yes, this is God. This is the way He is.

Hard to comprehend, isn't it? Maybe you ask—*When will God bless me?* Well, I ask you this—*What do you think the blessing is? A gift, some kind of favor?* Maybe this explanation will help. Let's say there is a homeless person and you give him bread. He eats it and maybe feels satisfied for an hour. But let's say that instead of giving him bread, you teach him a skill. After he learns the skill, he will be satisfied, not just for an hour but for a lifetime. Knowing a skill, he gains back his dignity and self-respect. And it changes his life.

It's the same with God. God can give us many things and multiple blessings—and He does this very often—but if He teaches us how to live in this world, how to go out and realize our hopes and dreams, we are much better off. We are not helpless; we will be victorious. That is why God gave us His Holy Spirit—the powerful source of all our blessings.

Chapter 3

God's Gifts

God's gifts are not like the rewards of this world, and God's words are not like the pronouncements of this world. When you are a child of God, you have His Spirit and His inheritance.

As soon as you accept what Jesus has done for you and welcome God as your Father, you will receive His gift—the gift of the Holy Spirit.

What is the Holy Spirit? The Holy Spirit is the very being of God, His breath, His very essence. It is what makes Him who He is. Holy Spirit is God's way of being, of thinking, of understanding, of loving. Holy Spirit of God is: word, love, wisdom, mercy, peace, faith, promise, power, knowledge, and so much more.

This gift is the very treasure that I mentioned to you before. The Spirit of God is the other side of you, the part you have been searching for. When you receive the Spirit of God in you, you will become alive for the first time. You will begin to think differently, talk differently, and walk differently. God said, "Seek the kingdom of God first, and everything else will be added unto you." And this is exactly what happens: You get God, and you get everything that God has.

God says that your eye has not seen and your ear has not heard; neither has your heart opened up to the things that God has prepared for you if you love Him. You can try to imagine the fabulous things that God could give you, but you won't be able because what He has in store for you is more than you can imagine.

And why is that? Because you don't know yourself, you don't know the very best things about yourself. Deep down inside you, hidden from you and the world, is something wonderful, something you were made for, the very best of you. The best of you will be revealed to you only by the Holy Spirit, for the Spirit searches and knows all things, the deep things of God.

How does this happen? If man has the spirit of man in him, then he knows the things of man. But the things of God are known only by the Spirit of God. From God, you will receive not the spirit of this world, but the Spirit that is of God. If you have the Spirit of God in you, you will know the things that are freely given to you from God.

In other words, if you have the Spirit of God in you, you will know the deepest things of God, including knowledge of yourself.

If you live in His kingdom as a child of God, God is continually molding you and teaching you. You are still the one making choices, but God is making you knowledgeable so you know how to make the right choices.

First, God shows you who He is. And then He shows you who you are, what your passion is, what you have been created for, and where you are going. You have to find out what you been created for, and then you must pursue it. No one can tell you what kind of life you should live because no one else really knows what God has created you for.

If you have God's Spirit in you, God will communicate with you. The people living just in this world will never have this privilege because, as much as we don't understand the path of the wind or the mysteries of deep space so without God's Spirit, we can't understand God's way. The people of this world will not receive an understanding of the Spirit of God because it is foolishness to them. Everything from God is hidden from this world, and this world will never, ever understand God's gift to His children.

The people of this world will never know the voice of God, they will not understand God's wisdom, and they will never get God's power. They will never know the way Adam and Eve walked with God, and they will never know that experience for themselves. They will never know the kind of peace and joy that comes from being with God. They will never know all the privileges that God has waiting for them. Without God's Spirit, they will not understand the anticipation and excitement of getting up each morning and wondering—What marvelous thing is God going to show me today?

You ask—*Why does everything that God has have to be hidden from this world?* We are God's children, and He wants to share His gifts with those who are His children only.

Let's just say that when a person creates something priceless, he wants to put his signature on it, he wants to tell everyone that this wonderful thing belongs to him. When a designer designs a new dress or an architect designs a new building or a scientist discovers a new star, each wants to put his or her own name on it.

So it is with God. God wanted to place His signature on His creation, and He did it in the following way: There is a space inside us that only the Holy Spirit can fill. If the Holy Spirit is not there, that space feels empty, like a void. If the space remains empty, everything from God is hidden; but if the space is full with the Holy Spirit, we understand the deepest things of God.

We are God's whole being, and we are precious to Him. He put His very being into us. After Adam and Eve sinned, He did not give up on us. He sent His Son to die for His creation and felt pain and sorrow when Jesus died on the cross. Don't you think that God would want to have His signature on His creation? Wouldn't you?

Have you ever spent time with a sick child? When he was healthy and got into trouble, perhaps you got angry. But when he became sick, you were heartbroken. When you saw him in pain, you cried and asked God to give you his pain, instead, so he would not have to suffer. After you felt his pain, your love for him grew deeper.

It's the same way with God. When Adam was with God in Eden, God loved him; but after Adam sinned, God loved him even more. He sees and feels your pain in the same way, and because He can't help you, He is in even more pain than you are. He wants to set you free and help you. But you don't believe Him, and you don't trust Him. God says to you, "How often I have longed to gather my children together, as a hen gathers her chicks under her wings, but you were not willing." In another place, He says, "Can a mother forget the baby at her breast and have no compassion for the child she has borne? Though she may forget, I will not forget you. See, I have engraved you on the palms of my hands; your walls are ever before me."

The walls God is talking about are your fears of trusting Him, of coming to Him openly. When you feel afraid, you close off your emotions and are full of suspicion, so you create a wall around yourself. God is saying, "I see the wall behind which you are hiding from Me, and I am waiting for you, so your walls are ever before Me."

When God created this world and created us, He said, "It is good." He created good people for a good world. Why, then, are we so unhappy living in this good world? We are unhappy because Satan is trying to imitate the Kingdom of God by making us believe that we are getting things from God. He is feeding us with lies, fantasy, and illusion. We get hooked on dreams of this world, but those dreams will never become reality.

Kingdom of the Spirit is the only reality and truth that have ever existed and will ever exist. To understand this kingdom, we have to dig deeply into the unknown to us; we have to dig into the Holy Spirit. If we build our dreams on the foundation of reality and truth, they will never fail, and they will become our true joy, contentment, and satisfaction. We will never look for anything else.

Word of God

Jesus is a word of God. Everything God created He created by saying a word. Everything coming from God's mouth is His word. Why did He choose His word to come to this earth? He chose the Word because He wanted to teach us the truth.

When you get the Holy Spirit, your eyes will be opened right away. People say—*The Bible is not from God; human beings wrote the Bible.* But the words of God in the Bible are hidden from this world because the Bible is written only for the children of God. The Bible is written for those who are already with God, who have the Holy Spirit in them. These people have already made the decision to go back to God—and their eyes have been opened.

Throughout this book, you will read passages that paraphrase the Bible, that illuminate the Bible, but do not quote it exactly or give specific credit to certain verses. That is because this book is a conversation about God rather than a scholarly work. Nonetheless, you will recognize that these truths are based on Biblical teachings and revelations—and they will resonate in your heart.

Jesus came into this world as a poor son of a carpenter. He could have come here as a king. But He wanted to relate to people who were in need so He became poor. Similarly, Jesus will come to you in the way that you need so that He can meet you where you are, so He can understand you and relate to you. It is very crucial that you search out the word of God, the Bible, by yourself. The purpose of this book is to show you the way to the truth, but you are the one who will be spending private time with God and discovering yourself on this road to freedom.

The deepest secrets for a happy and successful life can be found in the Bible, but they are hidden from this world so that thieves don't get hold of them and use them for the wrong reasons.

When I was a little girl, I had a book about an angry and mean little boy. This boy ran around the neighborhood screaming at other kids. He forced himself on everyone, and no one wanted to play with him or give him anything. The boy went home crying and complaining to his grandmother about his misfortune. His grandmother was a wise woman who said to him, "I will tell you a secret; I will give you a magic word. And every time you say this magic word, you will get whatever you want. When you use this word, you have to smile because otherwise it will not work."

The boy was very anxious to try his magic word. He went up to the first boy he saw and said to him with a smile, "Will you let me play with you?" And then he added the magic word: 'please.' The boy was so pleasantly surprised at what he heard that he responded immediately, "I'd love to play with you, and you can play with my toys too."

This is what the Bible is all about. It's full of magic words, words that disperse into the atmosphere when spoken and make things happen, make magic. The word of God is powerful, sharp, and alive, piercing into the soul and spirit, and performing what it is intended to do. You find the deepest secrets for a happy and successful life in the Bible. The Word of God will teach you, heal you, give you hope and strength. It will give you your dignity back.

People say—*I read the Bible, and I don't understand.* You don't yet understand because you are not a child of God; you don't yet have the Spirit of God in you. To explain this concept, think of yourself as a parent. Do you give all the best you have to people you don't know or those who couldn't care less about you? Rather, you save your best— your time, your resources, your efforts—for your children and other members of your family. It's the same way with God. He intends the Bible for His children.

You may say—*I will buy the Bible, I'll read it, and then if I like it, I'll decide whether to accept God's invitation or not.* God does not work this way. God does not give His treasures away to those who do not want to be with Him. Would you? First, you have to make your decision, go to God by faith, and accept His salvation. Then you will understand the Bible, and everything in it will be yours.

Love of God

God is love. Love never fails. Love is the key to everything. If you apply love, you will always win with everything you do. Many people have misconceptions about love. Most of us are afraid of applying love because we think we might become victims, that people will take advantage of us. But this is not true. Jesus said, "I send you forth as sheep in the midst of wolves; be you, therefore, as wise as serpents and harmless as doves." Being with God, you will learn the only one pure and true love, and you will gain that wisdom and understanding. When you apply love together with God's knowledge, you'll be blessed and so will everyone around you. If you apply love, God will always reward you.

Of all of God's gifts, love is the biggest and the most important. When you get to know God, you will know that everything God does is done with love. First of all, God loved us before we loved Him. And because He loved us, He sent His Son to die for us. He sent Jesus to die for us, knowing that we might or might not accept Him as our savior.

There is something very interesting about love. When we apply it, it is noticeable or very apparent to the recipient. A person with God's Spirit is very sensitive to love and recognizes it right away. On the other hand, if love is not applied, he will recognize that as well.

Let's say that your mother is in the hospital. She calls you and asks you to bring her a nightgown from home. You really don't want to go because you have other plans for the evening. But you feel you have to, so you change your plans to visit your mother. By the time you arrive, you feel angry, restless, and resentful, and she can sense it. Essentially, you've wasted your time and hurt your mother's feelings. Instead of making the situation better, you've made it worse.

But if you'd had a loving attitude and offered your time with love, you would have gained more than you can imagine. You'd feel happy, your mother would appreciate your kindness, and maybe your visit would give her encouragement to make it through her illness.

It is very important that you see the difference here because this will answer a lot of your confusion. When someone is doing something for you, you need to recognize what his motives are. If you know his motive, you will know his intention. And you will know the intention by the results. When love is applied, you will experience positive feelings of peace, joy, and contentment. When it is not, there will be a destructive sense of confusion and anger.

A friend of mine asked me once, "Should I do something for my girlfriend for Valentine's Day?" I told him he certainly didn't have to do anything, but if he wanted to have a girlfriend and companion, he'd better do something. The next day he told me he had taken my advice and invited his girlfriend to a nice dinner. The results of this date will depend entirely on his motives.

Why do people stop loving each other, and why do they get divorced? They stop loving each other because they try to possess each other. True love has to be free. We always dream of meeting the love of our heart, our soul mate. We search for this person all of our lives, and then when he or she comes along, we destroy that relationship.

For example: You meet someone, and there is sparkle and an attraction between you. For a few dates, you have a great time getting to know each other. Both of you are on your best behavior. Love starts to grow between you. Meanwhile, your hope and vision for perfect love is growing too.

Then one day, the problems start. You want to control, you want to change the other, and you want everything your way. Slowly, you begin to discover new things about each other that don't match your vision and your dream. It's not what you imagined in your picture of perfect love.

So you start demanding that the other person be the way you want him or her to be. You try to change and restrict the person. What you are really trying to do is surround the person with bars and make him or her your prisoner. You are starting to act like a terrorist in your own home, towards your own family member or friend.

Instead of having the friend and lover you wanted, you have an angry person just waiting to blow up with revenge. Then maybe each starts to yell and argue, to punish and humiliate, each trying to get his or her own way. Perhaps one person starts compromising to have peace in the home, but instead of having peace, he is slowly shrinking. The bitterness in him is growing, and before he knows it, he hates the other as his enemy because he feels he is jail.

Love is a choice—either you want to love, or you don't. If you want to love the other, you need to give him freedom, to let him be who he is, to let him like what he likes, to let him do what he likes to do. This is the only way you will have true love. You may ask—*What about me? Don't I have something to say?* Yes, you have to be free in love as well. You can't give yourself up for the other.

The only way to have a happy partner and friend is to respect the other and treat him with dignity. Remember that we all have personalities and characteristics quite different from one another. We are able to communicate about our differences and need to make a point to understand each other. I tell you something, if you want a friend and lover for life, you need to stand by him through the bad times, encourage him, and believe in him. And he will love you forever.

It is very important that you understand how love works, so you don't waste your energy and time. God says that love is the most important of all of His gifts. So everything that you do, you must do with love. Otherwise, your efforts mean nothing.

God says that if you give everything that you have for somebody, even your life, but do it without love, you do it for nothing. If you donate a million dollars to charity, but your motive is recognition and popularity, you do it for nothing in the eyes of God. Your giving must have the right motive—the motive of love.

What is happening in the spirit? If you give the million dollars with love, because you want to help the organization, you give from your heart. Your million dollars will come back to you and multiply. It's like planting a seed: You put the seed in the ground, and after a little while, it grows. This is a spiritual law of God.

In the same way, if you love someone for his money, he will never love you back, and you'll find your hold on his money is very tenuous. But if you love him for himself, you will receive not only his love in abundance but his money also.

You ask—*What is this big secret about love?* We look for it, we search and want to get it, but somehow we are failing. The more you give up for someone, the more you sacrifice—the more you will be loved for it. Jesus said that the perfect love is when you give up your life for the other. If you want to love someone and be loved, you have to give up something for this love. If material things are more important for you than the love for other, then your love is not worth much.

I see it all the time: A man asks a woman for a date. He wants her to be a jewel for him, but he wants her for free; he is not willing to give. Then he wonders why she does not love him. Once I saw a movie about a woman who had been saving money all her life to buy a house for the day she would be married. One day, she gave up all her money to save someone she sincerely loved from his trouble. Then she left his country, and he did not know the sacrifice she made for him.

I thought—Why she is doing that? She might not see him ever again. Was it worth it? Then I realized: If you want to live a full, happy, meaningful life, you need to sacrifice even if it is in secret. A soldier giving up his life for his country, a parent working two jobs to raise her children, a doctor traveling through a snowstorm to help someone in need, a husband giving up his sporting event to please his wife with a surprise dinner, a mother staying up all night with her sick child—all of these people are sacrificing themselves for the sake of love.

When was the last time you sacrificed for somebody? Do you wonder why your life is so meaningless? When you give your love, it is worth a lot, but whatever you give in silence, in sacrifice, is worth the most.

We have a disease going on here in America. We don't want to show people that we are trying to please them. We think they will take advantage of us and not respect us. So we go out of our way to look self-contained and not interested. Why are there so many divorces and so many lonely people out there? Because we do not want to put out any effort for the other. If we give from the heart, we gain more than we give because we are giving with good motives. We are giving for love. If we are not giving any-thing, we are not going to get anything back.

This is a law of love. What you give, you will get. When you put a seed into the ground, a flower will grow. Our lives work by the same law. When you start giving, then you will get back.

The next time you do something for someone, apply a little love, and see what happens. You will see a miracle.

Voice of God

When you get God's Spirit, your ears will be opened. People ask me—*How can anybody hear the voice of God? Who do you think you are that God is talking to you?* Let me tell you: You will never know the voice of God, the thrill of it, until you are with Him.

Let's say that you just bought a DVD player. You assemble everything and follow the instructions so you can watch a movie. But the picture does not come up. You get frustrated because you don't know what's wrong or why it's not working for you. You may want to give up. But if you show a little patience and read the instructions again, you discover that one crucial little wire is missing, and this is why you cannot make a connection. You return to the store for the missing piece, install it, and settle back to watch a movie on your new DVD player. And now you see the movie in a wonderful new way, with powerful sound, intense colors, and a panoramic view.

Likewise, when you find that missing piece in your life and you get connected to God, you will see things that were hidden behind the frames, hear things you've never heard before, and realize possibilities that were not there for you before.

What is wrong with our world that we are not able to see ahead, to dream, to imagine, to create? With God, everything is possible. In this world, you entertain thoughts that cause you fear and confusion, but with the Spirit of God in you, you will begin to have good, happy, positive thoughts that give you hope. You will not be afraid to dream anymore. So you will start to dream. And dreaming will offer you many opportunities to do something creative and positive. The Holy Spirit will open up your mind, and you will see. And when you see, you will be able to do. You will try, and you will accomplish. You will keep on going, and nothing will keep you from trying, no pain, no disappointment, and no resistance from other people. If anything stands in your way, you will kick it aside. You will be a giant; you will be powerful; you will be able to move mountains. You will be a winner.

You see, my friend, you have to give yourself a chance. And when you do, you will never be sorry. Go back to God and ask Him for the connection. He is the missing wire.

Wisdom of God

The smartest person in the kingdom of the world is just tapping the beginning of God's wisdom. Can you imagine?

The least significant wisdom of God starts with the highest wisdom on earth. Researchers say that we human beings use only a small percentage of our brains. This situation makes me think, since I know that God does not create anything without a reason, why do we have such big brains, and why are we using only a small portion of them?

Have you ever heard the statement, "Use it or lose it"? If it weren't possible to use our entire brain, wouldn't it simply shrink? I believe our brain doesn't shrink because we are inherently capable of using the whole thing. I see it this way: God's wisdom is so big that if we get hold of the entire thing, His wisdom would fill the entire brain. God's omniscient wisdom is what our large brains are made for. You don't think this is possible? With God, everything is possible. If we close down our brains and don't try to think big, we will miss what God has for us.

This also means that no one who belongs to the kingdom of this world will ever know the wisdom of God. God gives skillful and Godly wisdom; from His mouth comes knowledge. What is the wisdom of God? He created this world from his wisdom. Although it's almost unimaginable to us, God knows everything that goes on in this incredibly complex world. God has a plan and destiny for every single person, and He created us for this destiny. God says that wisdom makes a man's face shine and the very nature of his face shall change. If you have God's wisdom, you will be beautiful. Your face will shine with light.

Power of God

God says that there is no other power but God's. The power of God is the force that makes everything happen. Power is everything that the Holy Spirit does. By His power, God forgives sins. By His power, God gives you the Spirit of wisdom and revelation so you can understand who God is and how everything comes from Him. By His power, your understanding becomes enlightened so you know what you have been born for, you realize there is hope in your future, and you know the richness of God's inheritance for you. Just think of the exceeding greatness of God's power, a power without limits. Think of the meaning that this power has for you.

Jesus has power on this earth to forgive sins and set you free, power to build you up and lift you up, and power to make you victorious. He has the power to change you, to raise you up from a miserable and meaningless life to a happy and joyful life. God has power over this world, and He is able to give this power to you.

I remember when *Star Wars* first appeared in theaters and Yoda said to young Skywalker, "May the force be with you." This was a very powerful statement. Everyone wondered what it meant and was excited about it. Now, you don't have to wonder; the power is here, and it could be yours. Just reach out and take it.

You see, when you know who you are and who God is, at that moment, you will get the power. You will get the strength to stand up for yourself, and you will teach people how to treat you with respect.

There is something very interesting about people who don't crack up under pressure. They are our heroes: We want to follow them and be like them. Even in the worst situations in life, they do not listen to another's advice but simply do what is necessary. When they've done everything possible, they wait in silence. They do not scream, and they do not fight. They are not afraid because they know that there is a power, a force in the universe, that is working for them.

Every morning when you get up from bed, you go into the world and take care of your responsibilities. You do what is required of you. You cannot change anybody; you cannot force anyone to do anything for you. But if you apply the law of God, the power of God will take over and make things happen—and in ways far better than you ever imagined. You don't have to scream; you don't have to bang your head against the wall; you don't have to worry and lose sleep. You just need to trust God.

You may say—*That's easy for you to say; you don't know my responsibilities.* But I do know that your worry and anger will not help you in any way with your problems. Instead, they will cause you to become sick and weak and make mistakes under pressure.

You may say—*I want to be a hero. I want to be cool and collected.* And you can be. There is nothing standing in your way. You can have the power to be free.

There is no other power than God's power. We think that Satan has power over us, that he is in control of us, but actually he has no power whatsoever. How does he work then? He comes to you, and he talks to you. When you choose to listen to Satan's voice and follow, you destroy yourself. When you hear Satan's voice and listen, you form a picture in your mind, a picture of defeat and fear. Fear will come over you, and before you know it, you've become a prisoner of yourself and others. You become afraid to make a move and do what you want to do.

When Satan talks to you, you can choose to listen and do what he says, or you can choose not to. Why are you in pain? Why are you addicted to drugs or alcohol? Why is your life miserable? Because, at one time or another in your life, you listened to his voice and decided to do what he said. Satan talks to all of us, and he loves our misery so he chooses you and other people around you to mess with your life. You can listen and make your life miserable and allow others listening to Satan to make your life miserable as well.

You ask—*How come there are people in this world that have wonderful lives and everything they want? What kind of power do they have? And where do they get it?*

You don't need power to vegetate, to accomplish little, to stay in the same place. Think of children that come from rich families. Sometimes these children are never made to work for anything—everything is handed to them from their childhood on. They have no goals to meet, no dreams to fulfill. Have you ever tried to communicate with a person like this about his or her hopes and dreams?

There are people in this world who are sheltered from life's pain: They don't take any risks or take on any challenges. They are bored and live their lives by simply going through the motions. They may avoid pain, but they don't experience love either. They don't feel happiness, and they don't feel sadness; they don't cry, and they don't laugh. Their lives feel empty so they look for some kind of excitement. And sometimes they get into trouble because they look for excitement in the wrong places.

But I assure you, if you take chances and pursue challenges, if you look for the highest and the best, if you choose God, you will have more excitement than you'll ever need.

Mercy of God

Have you ever done something wrong to someone who was very dear to you? Perhaps you embarrassed and humiliated him or shattered his confidence and dignity. You did not mean to do it, but you did, and now you are sorry. You wish you could take everything back, but it is too late; you have lost your friend. You wish with all your heart that your friend would be merciful and forgive you, but your friend is hurt and not forgiving. This happens in our world all the time: an inability to forgive the wrong done to us, between people and between nations. Hurt is difficult to get over. But an unforgiving heart brings anger and bitterness, which eats away at us little by little. When we stubbornly cling to hurt and refuse to forgive, we ruin our lives and that of the other person.

My mother told me a shocking story I want to share with you. A long time ago, my grandmother's brother Ludwig had a married son. Ludwig's son was cheating on his wife, and after a while, the truth came out. His wife forgave him, but Ludwig, his father, did not. The son was no longer welcome to come home and visit his parents, not even on holidays. The son thought that, with time, his father would come to his senses and forgive him. But many years went by, and Ludwig did not change his heart. The time came when Ludwig was on his deathbed, and his son came to say goodbye. When his father saw him, he turned his head to the wall and, with the last breath left in him, asked his wife to remove his son from the room.

How can you understand this kind of story? Doesn't it just break your heart? Is there any justification for Ludwig's behavior? I cannot stop thinking about his son and the trauma of this rejection. Yes, he was guilty, but how could a father have so much hate for his son? If Ludwig had been merciful towards his son and forgiven him, there could have been a new beautiful relationship between them for many long and fruitful years. Instead, bitterness and regret followed them both through life, all the way to the father's deathbed.

God's mercy is not like that. Because of God's mercy, you have a second chance. Every time you screw up, God will forgive you, He will pick you up, He will love you, and

He will be merciful to you and give you another chance. God's mercy will melt your heart. After you experience all His goodness and mercy, you will wonder how you could possibly deserve this love that He gives you. That is why, after you know God's mercy, you will give him all of your life in return.

Hope of God

The kingdom of this world goes from bad to worse. The longer you live in this world, the more pain and disappointment you accumulate. After a while, you come to the conclusion that it is not worth it to be disappointed anymore. So you quit trying.

With God, you are in a totally different situation because God's ways are the opposite of the world's ways. In the Kingdom of God, you will go from good to better to the best. When you receive Jesus as your savior, God gives you hope right away. Hope will make you want to fight and not give up. Hope will stretch your imagination beyond human possibilities. Hope will make you see victory when everything seems to be in a terrible mess.

When the Apostles were behind bars in jail, they sang songs and worshipped God. Why? Because they knew that God was going to help them. Not only that, they had hope, a purpose for living; they had drive, a motive, a vision. And all of these things were stronger than pain, jail, and the darkness they were going through. When you have hope, vision, and drive, you can become a hero.

One time I saw a small woman who looked very weak to me. When a car fell on her husband while he was working under it, she lifted up the car bumper and saved him from suffocation. Where did she get her strength? She got her strength from her vision, her strong purpose to save him, and her hope to continue this life with her partner.

God's hope will give you power you never imagined you could have. God says that without vision His people will perish. Is it any wonder why so many young and old people are perishing in this world?

Peace of God

Jesus is called Prince of Peace because He brings peace to His children. The last thing Jesus said before he went away was "Peace, I live with you." In the dictionary, peace is freedom from disquieting or oppressing thoughts or emotions, a state of tranquility or quietness. There is no peace if you walk in the way of this world. It is a pillar of Jesus's teaching that we ignore the most. Everybody wants peace, but not everyone knows how to get it. Checking if you have peace is the way to know if you made a right decision, if you made a right choice, if your journey is on the right road. The doctor checks patients' body temperature to see if they are healthy; the mother checks the water temperature to see if it is comfortable for her baby's bath; the teacher checks the student with an examination to see if he is ready for advancement. The architect does the stress analysis to check if his design was done perfectly.

How do you check if your decision, the choice you made, was right? You simply check your mind for peace. If you do this every day, you will walk on the road of truth. The road to a happy and fulfilled life is the road of truth, which will always bring peace to your life.

As soon as up get up every morning and go about the day, you keep in your mind the checkpoint; you ask yourself a question—Is my mind at peace? What is in your mind at night when you put your head on the pillow? You check your mind because what is in it will tell you what kind of decision and choices you made throughout the day. If there is peace, contentment, and joy in your mind, this means you made good and healthy decisions. This will tell you that you are on the right road, that you are walking in the right direction. I call it the road of peace. When you are on the road of peace, you are on the road to success.

If you don't have peace in your mind, when your mind is in distress, when fear is tormenting you, you have to stop and find the cause; this is the checkpoint that something is very wrong and you have to find out what it is and correct it.

The peace of God surpasses all understanding. Jesus and the Apostles were in the boat, but Jesus was sleeping. A storm came up, and the Apostles were fearful they were going to drown. They awakened Jesus and asked Him if He didn't care that they were all about to drown. Jesus got up, lifted his arms, and said, "Let there be peace." And the storm calmed immediately; the sea became quiet.

Jesus said, "I give you my peace." As He was ascending to heaven, He said, "My peace I leave with you." Jesus came to this world to give you peace.

Faith of God

The Kingdom of God is all about faith. Without faith, it is impossible to please God. If you need faith, ask God, and He will give it to you. If your faith is as small as a mustard seed, you will be able move mountains. When you have just a little bit of faith, you can go to God and learn about Him. Then, you will be able to remove everything that stands in your way, all of your problems, all of your worries, all of your fears. Even the biggest problems that you see as impossible to resolve will be removed from your road to happiness and peace.

When you first go to God, you have a little faith. Perhaps you go to Him only because someone told you about Him and you decide to give God a try. Slowly, things start to happen that have never happened to you before as you to begin to open yourself up more and more to God. Your faith will grow, and when you see marvelous things happening, you will give yourself to God completely. Faith is a mystery. With faith, you will overcome the world.

The only way you can go to God is to go by faith. Faith is something that you do not see but something you believe will happen before it does. Faith is a wonderful thing because it gives you hope, patience, and vision. Faith is a gift from God.

I see over and over again that people go to God, go to church, and know they are His children. But they still live in the way of this world. They are stuck and will not give up their old ways of living. They have no faith. If they don't see and don't touch God's promises, they don't really believe in them. When I look at them, I feel so sorry because I see people who call themselves children of God but are not taking advantage of everything that God has for them. So they continue to live in this world crippled, wounded, and scared.

Because it is difficult to have faith in a world that often lies, we think that God acts in the same way. Maybe we think that He, too, lies to us sometimes. But without faith in His goodness, it is impossible to please God.

You are the greatest creation ever. Do you know this? Have you ever thought about this? Have you ever looked at yourself and appreciated who you really are? We are marvelous, and we are capable of great things—all of us, not only the next one, the other one, but also you yourself.

And all of us are equal. Oh, yes, we are different from each other too, but different fingerprints, different talents, different bodies don't make us unequal. We are all equal because we are all capable of dreaming and achieving our dreams. Ask yourself—*Why am I selling myself short? Why am I giving up on the biggest discovery of my lifetime, the discovery of myself, my greatness, and my wonders?* It is never too late to discover who you really are. As long as you are breathing, you are able to dream.

But you have to make a choice. If you want to be with God, you have to believe; you have to have faith. Otherwise, your salvation is for nothing, and you are wasting your time.

Someone said to me once, "When you have faith, you will win with God." You need to believe literally every word of God. And free your imagination.

Dreams

People ask me—*Why do you say that if you are with God you can dream and your dreams will come true?* Because when you are ready, God will give you a dream. You will know this dream is from God because it is going to be a dream that's out of this world. You won't be able to come up with this dream by yourself. This dream will be so big that maybe you will not be able to see yourself in it. God will talk to you about this dream, and after a little while, you will be able to grasp it. Then you will receive it into your heart.

You will see yourself having this dream and living with it. The thought of this dream will blow your mind away, and then you will decide to go after it.

At the same time, when you've made up your mind to go after your dream, fear will come over you. You will worry that your dream won't come true, that you will fail, or that someone will take it away from you. You'll worry that it might cause you pain and rejection to pursue your dream. You may even panic.

The point is this: You will not be able to do it by yourself. God will ask you to give this dream to Him. It is going to be frightening because you just took the chance, both emotionally and spiritually, and now you have to give the dream back to God. But, you must take that chance and let it go back to Him.

You have to trust God and tell Him that He can do it in His way and in His time. Once you do this, peace will come over you, and you will not panic anymore. Then you will discover that because you trusted God your creativity will flow like a river with energy and ideas. The work you create will be a work of art and not at all as basic as you originally planned it.

You will never go forward and will never mature if you do not patiently purse your dreams. When you overcome your fears and trust God, this dream will sharpen your faith beyond your imagination, destroy your fears forever, and set you free.

When I was a very young girl, I had my shallow dreams and hopes: the cars, the clothes, and the boyfriends. I came to America from a small Eastern European country when I was barely twenty-two years old because I wanted to be free. I had no idea what freedom was. I just wanted to run away from a country that kept me restrained. I thought and I dreamed—Oh, if I could just be in America; America is full of dreams and opportunities.

Then, one day, I arrived and finally lived the life of what we call "freedom" in America. It was a good freedom, and

I was happy for a little while. I had a dream to be free, but the freedom that God had in mind for me was something I had never imagined. I realized that true freedom was not America. True freedom was God.

When you really get to know God, you will be free, even if you are locked up in prison. Nobody will be able to take this freedom away from you, no Satan, no tyrant, no addiction, no pain. Do you know what I am saying? I am saying that the life of this world will not have a hold on you. When you are this free, you are free indeed.

So keep on dreaming, and you will find your freedom.

Strength of God

God says that you shall stand and feed on the strength of the Lord. Do you know how I see it? A boy goes to God, and when he touches God, strength runs through him like a jolt of electricity. In the twinkle of an eye, the boy becomes a giant with the strength of Hercules. This is the way of God: When you are weak, you are strong.

This idea is central to the ancient story of David and Goliath. A long time ago, there was a boy named David from the tribe of Abraham. Every day, David took care of the sheep on his father's farm, and his heart was full of faith and trust in God. He had a few strong brothers who were fighting in King Saul's army. God was with the nation of Abraham, and He was directing the people in their lives. At that time, there was a war between King Saul and the Palestinians. The Palestinian army had a terrible weapon—a seven-foot giant called Goliath. Goliath came out clothed in armor, screaming and shaking his weapon above his head. He challenged the soldiers of King Saul's army to fight; saying whoever would fight him and kill him would win the battle for his entire nation.

King Saul's soldiers were afraid of Goliath and fled one by one. David traveled to the army's position with food for his brothers, and when he saw what was happening, he said to King Saul, "Who is this uncircumcised Palestinian that he should defile the armies of the living God?"

David was not afraid, and he told King Saul that he would fight Goliath. Saul did not protest because no one else from his army would fight Goliath. King Saul tried to protect David with armor, but David was small, and the armor was too big for him.

When Goliath saw David, he laughed. But David was not intimidated. He took five smooth stones from the brook and ran toward Goliath, saying, "You are coming to me with a spear and with a shield, but I am going to you in the name of the Lord our God, whom you have defied. This day, the Lord will deliver you to my hand, and I will smite you and take your head from you, and I will give your carcass unto the fowls of the air and to the wild beasts of the earth, that all the earth may know that there is a living God."

David took a stone, placed it in his sling, took careful aim, and smote the giant in his forehead. The stone struck him with such power that he fell to the ground. Indeed, that very day, the young David killed the mighty Goliath. David was just a boy, but he knew who he was and who his God was. He knew the power of God. You can be strong, but if you don't know the power and wisdom of God, in reality, you are weak.

The more time you spend with God, the stronger you will get. Doubt and confusion will come back, but the more you trust God and seek Him, the more your doubt and confusion will recede. You will win over doubt and confusion when you keep your focus with your eyes on the author and finisher of your faith.

Once, I was haunted by fear. The fear was so strong that the picture of being already defeated was stuck in my mind. I did everything to get this picture out of my mind, but I could not. I was on vacation at the time. The tropical weather was beautiful, and everyone was having a great time around me, but not me. I was looking on the beautiful world with a picture of horror in my mind.

Right there in the hotel room, I got on my knees and quietly tried to remind myself of who I was. I whispered, "I am a child of God. I was redeemed by the blood of Jesus. Satan has no power over me. People can do nothing to me. I am victorious because I've been washed by the blood of Jesus. I don't belong to this world but to the kingdom of God. I am a child of the most High God, and He has everything in control."

As I was saying these words to God over and over again, I reminded myself who I was and who God was, and this knowledge gave me strength. In the middle of the afternoon, in this beautiful hotel room, I reminded myself of who I was, and I regained my freedom. I got up from my knees, put on my bathing suit, and went swimming. I was free.

You have to believe that God is here and now, and because He is here and now, you cannot be defeated; you cannot lose. Jesus has told us that He has overcome the world. Jesus has already won.

You say—*If He has already won, then what is going on in the world now?* Right now, God is gathering his children, He is educating us about His kingdom, and He is separating the wheat from the chaff. If you are a child of God and walking in His law of the Spirit, nothing is going to happen to you without God's knowledge

Before Jesus was to die on the cross, He stood in front of Pilate, and while they were accusing Him, He was silent. Pilate said, "Don't you know I have the power to crucify you and the power to release you?" Jesus said. "You have no power over me, except as it is given you from above."

Can you believe Jesus's statement? His total confidence? His utter freedom? He was in shackles, but He was free because He knew who He was, and this knowledge gave him strength to see His destiny through.

I see it like this. A baby eagle comes to his father and says, "I am trying to fly, and I can't do it; I fall down and get hurt. All I want to do is fly as you do." And the daddy eagle replies, "Don't you see me fly? You are my son, and if you see that I am able to do it, you know that you will be able to do the very same things that I do. And so, the baby eagle learns to remind himself of who he is every time he tries to fly. The day is coming soon when he will open up his wings and fly—just like his father. And he will be truly who he is.

Promise of God

The Holy Spirit is a promise from God. For all the promises of God are YES and AMEN. Whatever God promises you, it is going to happen, and this is for sure. You must see God as someone who always tells the truth. You cannot doubt; doubt is not in God's kingdom.

The most powerful promise from God to His children is the promise of salvation, of redemption, a promise to be free from the kingdom of this world and the promise to be made in the image of God.

We have been deceived and misled. The power and effects of sin, sickness, and death are our worst enemies. God guarantees our deliverance from evil forces and promises us redemption, to buy us back, to free us from distress and harm, to release us from blame and debt, to free us from the consequences of sin. After this is accomplished, He promises to make us in His exact likeness.

God gives you a promise that all your lost years will be given back to you. It works like this. Let's say you lose ten years of your life wandering, searching for truth. During this time, you do some stupid things that are destructive to your body and your relationships. Then one day, you find out the truth, that you are a child of God. When you come to God, He heals your mind and body, puts your life back together, and restores your very being.

When you walk in the way of this world, there are many dangers: harsh circumstances, poisonous addictions, fears, worries, stresses, and the constant presence of manipulation, cheating, and lying. You may have trouble sleeping, and sleep is designed to heal and rejuvenate your body and mind. Stress produces confusion and upsets your stomach. Fear makes you look at life warily and suspiciously. And when you feel afraid, you act defensively, fighting and yelling at others. Then your anger makes you feel guilty, and guilt makes you feel depressed. When you feel depressed, you don't take care of yourself, and maybe you drink or take drugs to mask the depression. All of these behaviors poison your body (and your mind) and make you sick.

But when you are with God, peace, hope, and a dream of your own will come into your life. You will have a reason for living, and the problems of this world will have no effect on you. That is when your body and your mind will be healed—and the healing will give you energy. When you get a taste of healthy living, you will have the strength to put away the things that are poisoning you, and slowly you will be restored. A healthy glow will come over your face, and you will have more strength than you ever had before. You will feel better than you felt when you were years younger. Of course, you are not going to be ten years younger, but you are going to look and feel that way.

Someone said to me that there are fifty-three promises in the Bible to every child of God. I haven't counted them, so I don't know if this is accurate. Maybe I could take some time to count the promises from my God to me, but what I know is enough for me: I am free, God loves me, and He wants to be with me. Everything else is just the icing on the cake.

God gave us a promise for eternal inheritance and eternal life. Can you believe this? To believe it or not is up to you. But if it's true, then it would be a real shame to miss it.

Knowledge of God

First you have to believe that God exists. Knowledge about God comes gradually, little by little, and as it comes to you, you will discover new things about yourself. Slowly, you will be transformed. As you become knowledgeable, you'll know how to make the right choices. God gives you knowledge so you can know Him, so you can understand Him. When you get to know God, you come to understand how He operates.

When you understand how God operates, the new world will be opened to you, a world of marvel, of astonishment, of excitement and amazement. It will be just as if someone removed a veil from your eyes and you see clearly. Then everything will become clear.

Chapter 4

From Kingdom of This World to Kingdom of God

You have just received God's Spirit, and you're thinking—*Great, my problem are over now. I am a new creature, I am pure and clean, I have new life, and I am starting all over again.*

This is not exactly the way it works. Yes, Jesus has done everything for you so you are, once again, a child of God, but this is just the beginning. Yes, you are a child of God, but there is some work that yet needs to be done in you. You need to be healed, cleaned, and forgiven of everything in your past. What God needs to do in your life now is take away your every pain and every wound so you can really start over again, pure and clean.

Pain and wounds from your past give you fear. And fear is your worst enemy. Fear stops you from reaching out and taking what is yours. When you are fearful, you feel paralyzed and afraid to go into the world and take everything that is there for you. This is Satan at work, try-ing to put fear into you. When you're afraid to get hurt, you get confused and feel timid. You are not able to live the life that you are meant to live, the life that God has created for you.

The answer is to get fear out of your life. This is the most important thing you must do. You have to make a commitment that every moment from this day forward you will strive to remove fear from your life.

You ask—*How do I get fear out of my life?* The answer is simple: You must become like a child. Yes, as simple as a child. Children are very interesting little people—we grownups have a lot to learn from them. Have you ever observed children listening to a fairy tale? They are totally absorbed by a fantasy, like that of Sleeping Beauty and a Prince Charming who awakens her with a kiss. No matter how fantastic it is, children believe the story. They never ask how Sleeping Beauty could be awakened with a kiss after sleeping for a century. Or how she could possibly lie comatose in the woods without being eaten by animals. No, children believe what you tell them because they believe that the world is full of possibilities.

Children are different from adults in another way. They don't give up easily. Children fall many, many times when they are learning to walk, but this does not stop them from trying. They don't get disappointed; they are not afraid. They simply keep trying and falling until they succeed. Their ability to eventually walk is never a question for them.

God says, "There is no fear in love, but perfect love casts out fear because fear is torment. He that fears is not made perfect in love."

When we become like little children, we operate in love. There is no suspicion, and there is no doubt. Have you noticed how a child born into a happy and healthy family sometimes just flows through life? His only concerns are to love and to be loved, and he trusts that everything will always be okay.

This is exactly how our Heavenly Father wants us to live. He wants your only concern to be this: to be making sure that you are doing everything in love from your heart with good motives. After you have done what is expected of you, you can rest and wait for the positive outcome. In other words, you only need to put the right energy into it, and everything else will work for you. You can relax and enjoy your reward. That is how the kingdom of God works.

To help you understand the kingdom of God better, I'll tell you about a vision I had a long time ago. In this vision, I saw a big room, very nicely decorated. The room had a northern exposure so it was always dark, but big glass doors opened onto a white granite terrace and a beautiful landscaped garden, flooded with sun. Opposite the glass doors, a white cage with a bird inside hung in a corner of the room. The bird was very sad and did not sing because the room was dark and gloomy. I heard a voice saying to me, "This is how my children live when they don't know about Me."

Then I saw a hand lift up the cage and move it next to the window. The bird looked at the beautiful sun-flooded garden and loved what he saw. He began to sing joyfully. I heard the voice again, "This is how my children live when they know about Me but they have nothing to do with Me."

I saw the hand again, and this time it opened the cage door. The bird saw the opened door and stood at the edge of the cage. He looked to the right and to the left and didn't know what to do. He had never used his wings before because he had never been free. After wondering for a while, the bird spread his wings and started flapping them up and down, checking to see what his wings could do. Then his wings lifted up his little body, and he flew from the cage, through the opened glass door, and out into the beautiful, warm sunny day. For the first time in his life, he felt the warm sun on his body. The feeling was overwhelming, and he started spinning around, flying up and down and stretching his wings out as far as he could to expose his body to as much sun as possible. Then he turned around, looked back at the cage and the dark room, and knew he could never live like that again.

He looked at the sun and knew that the only thing he really wanted and needed was the warmth of that sun. He stretched out his wings and started soaring towards the sun. The big room, even the white granite terrace and beautiful garden, were left behind. Then I heard the voice again, "This is how my children live when they know about Me and are part of Me."

The door to your freedom is already open. You only need to take the chance, spread your wings, and fly. Or you can choose to sit in the cage with an open door.

We live in the cage because we are afraid of what others think of us. God wants to take your fear away by teaching you who you really are. God created you—and He is the only one who knows you. God wants you to know that you are perfect in His eyes. He created you to be beautiful, and that's how He sees you, in spite of your sins. He understands all of your pains. He wants you to be free. He wants to heal and clean and purify you. He knows that you have been born with a curse and that you cannot help the things you do and say. God understands you; He will take you in His arms, hold you, and carry you. He will help you focus and not pay attention to the opinions of others.

You know what it is like in this world. This world can hurt you with humiliation and shame. People may laugh at you when you make a mistake; they may point fingers and call you names. When the media finds dirt on somebody, it doesn't take long before it's all over the newspapers, radio, and television. Those doing the exposing don't stop to think about how lucky they are: their sins are locked up in the secret chambers of their hearts, and as long as nobody knows about them, they feel safe. And they feel safe to continue to point fingers at others. Jesus is different.

You cannot be afraid of people and what they think and say about you. They have no power over you unless you let them. You cannot please everybody. If you take a chance, people might laugh at you, but if you keep your eyes on Jesus, He will give you strength, and you will be able to ignore what everyone thinks of you.

Be revolutionary; stand up for yourself. Don't let people put you down; don't let them make you little. I don't care where you are or how you see yourself; if you give Jesus a chance, you will be victorious.

One day Jesus was passing a leper. He stopped, touched him, and healed him. Isn't this just incredible? In those days, people were frightened of lepers because of their contagious disease and ran away from them. They were considered dirty and contemptible. In this story, Jesus is teaching us about three laws of the Spirit. He stopped because he had compassion; He touched because he understood the leper's shame; and He healed because He knew the leper's pain.

God loves you as he loved the leper. He thinks you are beautiful, no matter what others think. He won't leave you or point fingers at you. If you are all alone and everyone else has abandoned you, He'll be right there with you.

You ask—*How do I know that God is always with me?* And I say—*This is something that you will not truly understand until you are with Him.* But I tell you that you will come to know that God is with you when you do something stupid once again, when you are so broken and ashamed that you don't want to get out of bed again. When you feel you cannot look another person in the eye, when the world looks dark, this is the very time that you can depend on God. He will be there. Loving you. Holding you. Caring for you. Yes, you will know that He is there with you.

You might think you won't cry because maybe you're a macho man, but inside the four walls of your bedroom, behind closed doors, you might cry like a baby. And for the first time in your life, you will be free, you will be opened, and you will be happy.

If you think you can disappoint God so much that He will never forgive you, you are wrong. Jesus came to this earth and died on the cross for someone just like you. Someone who is in pain. Someone who is in shame. Someone who is hurting. God said, "I didn't come to save perfect people; I came to save the sinners."

When you do something stupid, don't hide—but run to Him and ask Him to forgive you. He will clean you and make you pure again. Because of the blood of Jesus, you have this right. Maybe you say—*This is great, I can sin and do whatever I want, and as long as I go back to God, I will be clean and forgiven.* Yes, this is true because the Law of the Spirit is working with you in the following way.

If you go to God, He gives you His Spirit. And He begins to take all of your desire for sin away. Not right away, but slowly, little by little. When you are with God, you have to shift your priorities, stop thinking about your old habits and sins, and concentrate on the kingdom of God. Seek Him first, and run after Him.

You ask—*Why do I have to seek Him and run after Him? Isn't Jesus freely available to me?* And I answer—*Salvation is free, but Jesus must be sought.* Jesus paid a very big price for us. He shed His blood and was humiliated for us. When Jesus was dying a shameful death on the cross, God was so devastated and in so much pain that He had to turn His face away. He could not look anymore. Jesus had been with God for all eternity and knew God's presence. When God turned His face away, Jesus felt it in His very soul and cried out, "Father, Father, why have You forsaken Me"?

When Jesus died, God was in so much in pain that the sun disappeared, the wind and rain raged, and it was black as night in the middle of the afternoon. It was a dark and ominous day, just like the day that Adam and Eve sinned and had to leave the garden.

If you need Jesus, you are going to have to search for Him, and you are going to have to run after Him, just as you would run after the most desirable lover.

At this point, maybe you are thinking that you are not going to run after anybody, that this story is not worth much to you. Then I guess your life is not worth much either.

Maybe you say—*Nobody is going to tell me what to do. My life is mine, and I'll live it just the way I have been and the way I want.* So I say—*Go ahead, put the book down and try to work everything out by yourself. Keep on trying and keep on falling down.* But I tell you, day after day and month after month will go by. Before you know it, twenty years of your life will go by, and you'll still be in the same place, continuing to try and continuing to fall down. I suspect that after twenty years of trying, you are only going to be more hurt, more confused, and more bitter.

I think you know what I am saying now. You have to learn about the love and compassion of God; you have to learn how to give up your old way of thinking and living. You have to learn to be open to new possibilities and to start believing in new things. You have to learn about the kingdom of God, who God is, who you are. And when you start to learn these things and live your new way with God, you will face your first challenge. Fear will come over you, telling you that you are imagining things and that this is just a fantasy.

To meet this challenge, what is going to keep you in focus?

Vision

Vision will keep you in focus. As soon as you go to God and get His Spirit, God will give you a vision. God said, "And it shall come to pass that I will pour out My spirit on people; people will prophesy, see dreams and visions."

What does this mean? When the Spirit is poured out on you, you will know deep down inside your being that something extraordinary has happened to you. You will feel excitement, contentment, and peace, and you will know that you are a child of God. You might not have a vision exactly like mine. We are all the same, but God is working with each of us differently. But you can look for a pattern as each of us has to go through similar things.

When I received God into my life twenty years ago, I was tired and worn out from searching. When I finally received Jesus as my savior, I expected to understand the Bible right away. But the Bible still did not make any sense to me. In a moment of despair, I felt that nobody wanted me, not even God. I cried—and fell down on my bed from exhaustion. All of a sudden, I became aware that I was having a vision. I was not sleeping; I heard water running in the bathroom on the other side of my bedroom wall and my sister talking in the other room. I was awake, but I was seeing things and experiencing things that were not part of my normal life at all.

Inside my eyes, I saw a desert, and I was standing right in the middle of it. I looked around and saw sand all around me, all the way to the horizon. Far away, almost next to the horizon line, I saw a castle and a long, long line of people waiting to get into it. The castle seemed to be made of a brown metal, and there was a wall around it with four towers on each corner. The roof extended like a half-sphere over the entire castle, and water surrounded it. A bridge over the moat led to the entry door.

I stood at the end of the line, waiting for my turn to get into the castle. I had no idea what we were all waiting for, but I felt curious. When my turn came, I passed over the bridge and came to a tall door, so tall I could not see over the top. I stood in front of the door, which was made from two bronze pieces that met in the middle. There was no lock, and suddenly the doors start sliding: one to the right, the other to the left. I looked inside, and it was dark except for a steam of light coming from an opening in the center of the high ceiling. Light was falling on God, seated on a white granite throne in the middle of the room—falling on his white hair, his white robe, his shoulders, and his arms as they rested on the arms of the throne. I could not see the face because it was in shadow. When the door opened completely, light from outside fell on the castle floor in front of me. I walked inside, fell on my face in front of the throne, and I cried, "Please God, forgive me for my sins." God said to me, "Go to My Son first." And all of a sudden, I was outside again, behind the door. I sat on the step and wondered: Where I am going to find His son?

I looked around and saw small houses spread out around the desert. I knocked on the door of the first house, and the house start shaking. Jesus opened the door and said, "Go away; your faith is shaking." I started to beg him, "Please don't send me away. He told me to go to You first, and I don't know where else to go."

Then Jesus told me to come in. The house was very simple; there was only one room with a table in the center. There was no bed, but on the left wall, a fire burned in a large fireplace. We both sat down right in front of it. Jesus was on my left, holding my left hand. There was a love and peace surrounding us that is not possible to describe. After a long silence, I spoke, "Could you please tell me if my dream will come true?" He looked at me and said, "I don't know, but we can ask the Father." And He started praying in silence. After a little while, He looked at me again and said, "The Father isn't telling me, but let us go to Him and ask Him."

We left the house, traveled around the castle wall, across the bridge, and were soon standing in front of the bronze door. The door opened, and I saw a shadow in front of me, a shadow of myself as a child, reaching only as high as Jesus's hips. Again, I fell on my face in front of the throne and cried, "Please forgive me for my sins." By this time, Jesus was standing next to the Father at His right hand. Jesus said to the Father, "This is Your daughter. She was lost, and she is found again." God replied, "I believe You because You are My Son." Then Jesus added, "She wants to know if her dream is going to come true."

I was still lying with my face down when I heard Jesus speak to God in my behalf. I thought—God can say yes, or He can say no, or He can say maybe. I stopped breathing and moving; I was waiting for an answer and didn't want to miss anything. Somehow, I found myself standing in front of the throne, and God reached out with His right hand and put His fingers under my chin. Then He stretched out His arm toward the door and said, "GO AND GET IT."

The voice came out from His mouth, and the long-awaited answer made me feel completely paralyzed and lightheaded. A scream voluntarily came out of me, as if something inside me needed release. And I felt a huge sense of relief. I knew that the door had opened because I saw a shadow on the floor in front of me again. I slowly backed out toward the door, and God added, "Go and visit My Son sometime."

Then I found myself sitting on the step behind the door again, and I cried with Jesus standing next to me. When I was done crying, I looked up and could not believe what I saw. The land surrounding the castle was not a desert anymore but a lush green place with birds, trees, a river, and fields of growing wheat. Jesus took my left hand and led me down a dirt road next to the river. I was feeling so peaceful, loved, and contented that I wanted to be with Him forever. I said, "I don't want to visit You just sometimes; I want to be with You forever." He said, "I will be with you always. I will give you my comforter, the Holy Spirit."

As suddenly as it had begun, my vision came to an end. But the words—GO AND GET IT—were still ringing in my ears. I did not understand those words. Go and get it? What did that mean? I knew that all of my life I had been trying to realize my hopes and dreams, but whatever I had tried, I had failed. I had not yet been able to "go and get it."

Eventually, I left those words from God alone. I knew that someday I would find out what they meant. In the meantime, I knew that I had received a special gift. I knew what was at the end of my journey here on earth, and the victory and freedom were waiting there. I knew that, regardless of what happened from the time of my vision to the day of my victory, I would survive until I was free.

It did not matter what was ahead of me—the pain, the broken dreams, the defeats and humiliations—because I was going to be victorious.

After the vision, I picked up the Bible, and for the first time in my life, I understood. Every word was like magic. I could hardly wait to get home from work every day and find out more and more about my Father and my God in heaven. I wanted to know all the wonderful things He had in store for me.

The Law of the Spirit and the Law of This World

You have to see the difference between the law of the Spirit and law of this world because if you understand the difference you will see everything in a new way.

God's law of the Spirit is totally different from the law of this world. We live in the kingdom of this world and don't understand the law of the Spirit. Without the Spirit of God, the people of this world will never understand the law of the Spirit. They can never get hold of it. It seems like mere foolishness to them.

However, it is not that simple. Think of all the years that you have lived in this world with its evil ways, and no matter what you have been and what you have done, this way of life and this law have been the only way you've known. What God needs to do in you now is to rid you of bad habits and teach you new good habits.

God wants us to be free. And God wants to teach us how to live successfully in this world. When we become children of God and belong to His kingdom, we still have to live on this earth. To live successfully in this world, you have to learn the law of the Spirit.

You may ask—*Why do I need to learn this law? I prefer to learn from my own mistakes. If someone needs to tell me what to do and how to live, I'm no better than a zombie.*

But experience teaches us this is not true. In a very simple way, living in the kingdom of God is like driving a car well—well enough to feel competent, comfortable, and confident.

Let's say a father hands the car keys to his teenage son and says, "Get in the car and go." Wouldn't the son question him? "How? I don't know how to drive." Then his father tells him, "Just go ahead and start. As you drive, you'll make a few mistakes, but you'll learn. You need to be independent and learn for yourself, so I won't tell you what to do."

So the son gets in the car, manages to start it, and goes down the street. But traffic is coming towards him. He doesn't know what to do, which way to turn, or where to look first. He's definitely having difficulties so he starts to get upset and feel fear. His heart pounds, and he starts to sweat. In this situation, he cannot enjoy driving—or the scenery or the journey. He's just worried and tense, afraid that he'll hurt himself and others.

Of course, we know the solution here. The right thing to do is to get some instruction first: learn how to drive the car, learn the driving laws, and then drive with an instructor to guide you for a little while. The instructor tells you what to do, when to stop, how to back into a parking space, and how to merge onto the freeway. After learning all of this, you're ready to drive on your own. Gradually, you lose your fear and start to love driving. It's fun because you feel confident, knowing that whatever happens, you'll know how to deal with it. You enjoy getting there, and you enjoy the view along the way.

God wants you to enjoy driving through life. Learning His law of the Spirit is the key.

So what is the law of this world, and what is the law of the Spirit? The law of this world consists of everything that you do and everything you believe in, the things that you attempt to get by with in this world. For example, maybe you believe that if you love someone, he or she better love you back or you will make the person love you. Maybe you try to make people love you by making them feel guilty. If someone hurts you, maybe you get even and hurt the person back. To get somewhere in this world, maybe you manipulate, lie, compete, and fight. If someone doesn't like you, maybe you try to change who you are to please him or her.

You were born into this law. Generation after generation lived by this law, and no one ever thought to change it. Until Jesus. When Jesus came into this world, people heard of a new and different law for the first time, the law of the Spirit. It was so different and so incredible that people were completely astonished by it. Jesus said things that were out of this world, things that did not really make any sense.

Jesus started teaching people about the kingdom of God, and one of the first things that He said was, "Blessed are the poor in spirit, for theirs is the kingdom of heaven," and then, "When I am poor, I am blessed."

From our knowledge of the law of this world, we could certainly object—*What is this? This is an astonishing thing to say. What could it possibly mean that when I am poor then I am blessed? It just doesn't make any sense.*

But let us analyze these statements. When a person is poor, he is unhappy because he is hungry. He thinks about food all the time and has no peace until he gets some. Jesus is saying that, from now on, if you want something so much that you feel you are very poor without it; then you are blessed because this is a sign that you will get it. It means that if you want something very badly, you will get it for sure.

Now let's try to think with this new law in mind. What is it in your life that you want so much that without it you are very poor? If you have God's Spirit, this precious thing is exactly what you are going to get because this is the law of the Spirit.

Is this law of the Spirit so much different from the law of this world? The law of this world says that if you want something deeply, don't try to get it because you will be hurt, depressed, in pain, and you may not recover from your disappointment. The law of this world says: Don't get your hopes up because you will be disappointed.

You may ask—*Are you telling me that if I am with God and operating in the law of the Spirit, I can go after what I want, and I will always get it?*

Yes, that's exactly right. God says, "If you abide in Me and I abide in you, whatsoever you ask will be given unto you." Here's what the dictionary says about the word abide: to remain, to submit to, and carry out. God is saying, "If you remain with Me and submit to Me, you will have anything that you want."

You may say—*This is wonderful. I will finally have what I want?* Yes, I assure you that you will, but it will not happen right away. First, God wants to make you wise and knowledgeable. God wants to teach you so you'll know exactly what choices to make and why.

The other very important law of the Spirit is this: Whatever you sow you will reap.

Everything that you do in this life, the choices you make, are like seeds. If you make a decision and carry it through, you plant this seed, and it will grow in your back yard. You are going to live with the fruits of that seed to the end of your life, whether you want to or not.

This world acts as if it does not know about this law. If people knew about this law, they would not do the things they do. Think of the most extreme and terrible decisions people make: to murder someone. Maybe they don't care about the victim's life, or they feel it has less value than their own. The killer may think he's young, fast, clever, and able to escape the consequences. But the truth is, even if the killer escapes detection and jail, he will never be free. He will reap the punishment. He'll be in a jail of his own making until the end of his life.

On the other hand, if a person sows something good, that good will come back to him. Generosity of spirit, even when it involves personal sacrifice, always makes a person feel good.

The Bible is full of information about the law of the Spirit and the many ways it plays out in our lives when we follow its precepts. I cannot mention them all in this book. But I will say this: If you seek and then follow the law of the Spirit, you will be strong, powerful, wise, smart, healthy, beautiful, young, energetic, rich, happy, and peaceful. You will learn how to deal with this world and the evil in it.

Pain

It is very important to understand a few things about pain. Pain is what brings fear into our lives. We are afraid because we think we might end up in pain. Let me illustrate. The company you work for is laying people off. You just cannot lose your job. You're worried because you might lose your house or be unable to feed and clothe your children. You're worried because you think you can't handle the uncertainty. You're worried that you won't be able to recover from such a devastating experience. You're in pain.

But if you know the truth about pain, you won't be so afraid. Nobody likes pain, but if you understand it, you will be able to deal with it. In truth, pain is your friend.

When a woman finds out she is pregnant, she is happy even though she knows she may be sick and feel discomfort for nine months. But she does not think about the pain—she thinks about the change in her life, about the baby and the love the baby will bring to her life. She does not think about her pains; she thinks about her happiness—about the new and precious being coming into her life.

But when the mother is about to deliver her baby, she is in pain. Pain is telling her to get ready, to pay attention, to assume the right position. Pain is a sign of the birth to come—the birth that is bringing new life.

Likewise, when an athlete is training for the Olympics, he does not think about the long solitary hours of training, the physical stresses, pains, and injuries, or even his nonexistent social life. He is thinking about winning the gold medal. He is thinking about victory.

You have to think about pain in the same way. Pain comes into your life because it is time for change. If you pay attention, you will discover that every time pain appears in your life, it means you are about to win. You have to find the source of this pain in your life, and you have to act.

Let's say the same pregnant woman doesn't know she is pregnant. She feels sick, and she gets fat so she takes pills to lose weight and other pills to feel better. She is panicking and acting the wrong way towards the pain. And if she continues this way, she will lose the baby.

The worst thing you can do when you feel pain is to panic. First, try to find the source of the pain. Maybe a new change is coming into your life. Changes are scary and painful, but think like an athlete. Think about winning.

Maybe your life is full of boredom; maybe you're simply doing the same things over and over again. Maybe you've waited and prayed for change. Now that the time for change is here, you feel like panicking. The pain is simply telling you that change is coming. And the pain will give you a reason for love.

Once I saw a poster with a big red heart covering the background. A beautiful woman stood in front of the heart, holding a long, sharp knife in her hand. Blood from the knife and from deep cuts in the heart dripped onto the floor into a big pool of blood where the woman was standing. I know what the artist was trying to say here, but I was seeing something entirely different. I was seeing the heart of humanity, lying open and exposed to pain.

You think that your heart is protected inside your body, but actually it is vulnerable and exposed to everything that is going on in your life. And this is your biggest fear. The thought of going through pain and the fear of it are holding you back from living the life that you are made for. The degree of your fear tells you something. The more fear you feel, the more unhealthy your life is.

Why do we go through pain? For years I asked myself this question—Why do I have to suffer? Pain and suffering are not fun and do not leave fond memories. Pain can cut like a knife and leave you feeling sick and paralyzed.

I remember many times lying in bed, curled up in a fetal position in the middle of the night, trying not to scream from pain. I remember days of illness when it took all of my strength to crawl out of bed. I remember the darkness of night and my face covered with tears. In my pain, I longed to seek God's face. I would reach out, and in a quiet voice, I would whisper—Please Jesus, help me. And then, right at that moment, His love would come like a shower to wash pain from my crying soul, just as water washes away the dirt. My tears were no longer tears of pain, but tears of love, melting my heart.

Between painful nights, nights come when there is no pain, and life is fun again. Like you, I love fun, healthy days when the sun shines and children laugh. When I'm not in pain, I sleep through the night like a baby and get up in the morning feeling refreshed and rejuvenated. The day after a night like this is good and easy. I'm happy, and my face glows. But I think about the love of God that I missed, the love that passed me by because of my healthy and sound sleep. Which kind of night do I love the most? I'll take God's pure love any time, no matter the cost, no matter the pain.

Because of pain, I know God's love. God loves you all the time, when you are on top and when you are on the bottom. When everything is going well and there is no pain and no confusion, you don't even know that God is there with you. You feel you don't need God on your good days, but God is still there next to you. He is always working in you, whether you know that He is there or not.

God has different purposes for different people. Whatever your individual need is, this is the way God will personally lead you. If you are poor, God will become poor. If you are sick, God will become sick. If you are depressed, God will be depressed. He will walk in your shoes, and He will feel your pain.

When you get to know God's love, deep down in your very being, you'll know His love is with you forever, in good times and bad. When you know that God does not leave you in bad times and that He'll be there when everybody else in your life is gone, then you will understand that you can trust Him forever. Then you will trust Him with your whole life and let Him lead you through all your decisions and choices and challenges. God will be All in all things for you.

One day I asked myself—*Why do I need to be in pain to have God's love with me? If God is with me all the time, why can't I have His love with me all the time?* Then I decided that when I have a happy, healthy day, I would seek God in exactly the same way I did when I was sick. When you're sick, you feel no distractions from the outside; all of your senses and attention are focused inward to your spirit. That's why, when you're sick, it's easier to find God.

When you're happy, do the same: Close all your senses to the outside and look within, to your spirit. You will find God, and when you do, you'll discover that your pain will depart from you more often. And one day, it will be gone.

Knowing that God is always with my pain has made me very sensitive to other people. I can sense the pain of a bleeding heart right away, without talking to the person or knowing anything about his or her life. Sometimes I want to go to the person, take him or her into my arms, and say that I understand.

Yes, I love people, but I love God more. God gives me the kind of love I've never known before. From God's love, I learn how to love people in spite of their limits and their shortcomings. People are capable of love, but they are very suspicious. It is very hard to open up and communicate love to others since our love is not complete until we take away fear. Only God is able to give us the confidence to love one another with truth, purity—and without fear.

Loving people will often disappoint you. There are many demands in love, demands that are hard to fulfill. To be with someone, you need to compromise or make demands. God's love is not that way. When you are at your lowest, you will find out about the pure and precious love of God. When everyone has left you, when you feel shame and humiliation, when your heart is bleeding and your mind is tormented with the pain of jealousy, God's unconditional love will be there. Not next to you, not outside you, but deep down in your spirit, soul, heart, and mind. This is the kind of love you cannot know from another human being but only from God Almighty.

We often represent love as an arrow through a heart, but I would represent love instead with a bandage around the heart. True love always heals and never wounds. If you know God's love and learn how to love the same way, you will heal everyone you touch. No one will be able to hurt you; you will be like a pure ointment poured out in love—a vessel of the true love that comes only from God because only God's love is pure.

No one wants to be in pain; we prefer to run as far away from it as we can go. But if you are in pain, don't wait a single minute. While you are running, run straight to God.

Passion

Passion is the most beautiful word in the world, but everyone is afraid to touch it and talk about it. Passion means different things to different people. Maybe you don't know what your passion is or how to get it. But you know you want passion in your life; you know it's wonderful. Maybe you've gone after it many times but could not find that special thing that you were passionate about. And because you failed, maybe you stopped looking.

Let's say you have a mediocre job that pays your bills and you wait every week for the weekend to come. But what are you really waiting for? You are waiting for your death to come. When you look at yourself in the mirror, with honesty and truth and without fear, you see a person who has lost his life.

Perhaps you say—*You don't understand. I'm tired; I'm sick; I don't have the energy to search or fight anymore.* And I agree—You are sick and you are tired because you are depressed. You are depressed because you don't have a reason to live.

What you need is passion. Passion is a gift from God. Passion is a reward. It is a medal. It is a triumph. It is a victory. Do you know what it's like to be a winner, to be victorious, to finally arrive?

If you're sitting on your couch right now, feeling depressed and lost, and you don't know what victory is, let me tell you a story. Remember my vision and those enigmatic, mysterious words I received from God, GO AND GET IT?

At the time, I left those words alone because I didn't understand them. But I didn't forget them. My life was one big mess at the time, and I was falling deeper and deeper into confusion. I was trying to walk with God's Spirit and see His direction, but I was so anxious to realize my dreams that I was doing a lot of things on my own, with my own understanding. I was losing my fight for peace and freedom, and I was not able to stop the loss.

We live in constant pressure from this world. We think we have to make everything happen; the problem is we don't really know how. I was no different. I had searched for my passion for so long, trying different things, hoping

that each was my passion. I started five different busi-
nesses, and none of them worked. I worked very hard,
long hours; I studied and practiced until I had perfected
my knowledge about each of them. And when the time
came to open the doors and start running things, I was
not able to do it. Why?

I was working too hard at it, getting exhausted and
worn out. I was wasting my energy and my time. Because
each time, the thing I was pursuing was not my passion.

Finally, one day, I was at the end of my rope. No matter what I did, nothing got better for me; the situation just
kept getting worse. I was exhausted. I got on my knees
and I prayed, "What am I doing wrong, God? Show me
the truth. How come I am losing? I have your Spirit in me,
and I remember what You said in the Bible. 'It shall come
to pass that the Lord shall give you rest from your sorrow
and from your fear and from the hard bondage, which you
made yourself to serve.' So, God, why am I still losing?"

After a few minutes of silence, I heard a small, quiet
voice in my spirit. *Seek the kingdom of God first, and everything else will be added onto you.* This quiet, small voice
was not my voice. I am not smart enough to come up with
such a marvelous idea on my own. Those few words were
not words that human beings even think to say. I knew I
could not ignore them.

I understood what God was saying. He wanted me to
trust Him, switch my priorities, put everything else aside,
and seek Him first. I started analyzing my situation: I had

no job and no prospects, the money was running out, my personal life was going nowhere, and on top of everything else, I was depressed and sick. I realized—What more did I have to lose?

By trusting God completely, I had a chance to prove to myself that what God says is the truth. If God wasn't telling the truth, I didn't care; I wasn't going to lose much anyway. I had tried to do it all myself, and it had not worked. Now I was resigned. If I failed, so what? Once again, I would have failed. This was my analogy: I was prepared to take a chance and find out what God had for me. I became a gambler; I put my life on the line. If I was going to win, I was going to win BIG, and if I was going to lose, I was going to lose it all.

I took out the Bible and start searching, learning, observing, speaking to God, and waiting on Him, learning about His character and about His personality. The deeper I dug, the more I understood, and the more everything became clear. I was seeing parts of the puzzle come together like magic. Then one day, I stepped back and looked, and I saw. Finally, I understood.

That was in February. By May, I had a new job and had put a deposit down for a place on the waterfront. I put my condo up for sale the same day, sold it in two weeks, and then moved into my new place—the place of my dreams. All of this happened in two weeks, but this was not the end to my blessings. I had put God first, and my life was turning around. Little did I know that God had something even more dramatic in store for me.

A year later, on January 5, I awoke at three o'clock in the morning with all kinds of strange and wondrous thoughts coming into my head. The thoughts flowed with urgency, like a torrent that I could not stop, whether I wanted to or not. So I put on the light and began to write them down, line after line, writing densely on a single-spaced tablet, front and back. I wrote furiously, non-stop, for twelve straight hours. When my hand became cramped and numb, I started talking into a tape recorder. I recorded eight tapes all together, and when I was all done—about eighteen hours later—I was breathless, stunned, amazed about the experience I had just had. I had felt compelled to write and speak for hours on end, from a voice that was coming not from me but through me. The result is the very book that you are reading.

I had finally found my passion. Maybe my passion had finally found me. I had never thought it possible because, you see, I had never written anything in my life, and English is my second language. But I was writing and loving it. I was writing with love, and it was my passion. And I believe God had a reason for giving me—an ordinary person with little writing experience—these thoughts and this book. Speaking through me, He could speak directly, sincerely, without guile. With perfect innocence.

I finally understood what it meant to GO AND GET IT. When you get God, you get everything that God has for you. Everything is there for you; there are no limitations; everything is spread out on an open field. You just need to GO AND GET IT, just go and pick it up.

Let's get back to you now, my friend. If you look for God with all of your heart, with all of your mind, and with all of your soul, you will find Him. When you find Him, you will open a door to a most wonderful place. I am not even talking about getting to know the most High God, His love, His way, and His truth. I am not even talking about your dreams and your hopes. I am talking about your passion.

Passion is the gift that you will receive from God, something that will occupy your whole being, something that will consume you. You will become obsessed with it, but it will be a marvelous obsession. Your mind and creativity will be opened, and you will know the purpose for your life and for your being. You will work for hours, and when you are tired, you won't want to stop. You'll have something wonderful to accomplish that will occupy you to the end of your days. Your life will bloom. You will flourish and be full of life.

Just have faith! You will get your passion, but you will get it at the end of your journey to God after you have searched and learned, after you have asked forgiveness and been transformed, after you turned over everything in your life to God. After all of this, then you will have arrived. After all of this, then you will win, then you will receive your medal: your passion.

There is a trick about passion. You will not be able to get it on your own because it is a gift from God. When you try to get it on your own, you will fail because you won't know where to look and you'll look for it with the wrong motives. The thing that God has in mind for you to do is something that might never enter your own mind. You might not see yourself doing it because, by yourself, you are not capable of imagining it, much less doing it.

A friend of mine was a divorce lawyer. She worked with people that were going through a lot of bitterness and pain. She was making great money and accumulating many beautiful and expensive things. I saw her at a private party at the house of a mutual friend. She looked as if she was about to have a nervous breakdown; she was shaking and out of control.

At first, I thought she was sick. That was the only reasonable explanation for her behavior. Here we were, surrounded by our old friends, in a happy and friendly atmosphere, and she was loud and very angry. I took her aside and asked her for an explanation. To make a long story short, after talking to her and trying to understand her, I found out that her job was completely wearing her out. I said to her, "You cannot go on like this; you have to quit." She replied, "How am I going to pay my bills? This is the only thing I know how to do. I can't take this pressure; just leave me alone." And she stormed out of the room.

I saw her one more time that evening. She came up to me and said, "I have to go home with someone tonight. I need to relax; I am under too much stress." And then she went to find someone—anyone—to go home with.

Talk about human self-destruction! My friend was afraid, and that is why she allowed herself to sink this low. She still had a chance; she still could have called upon the Lord, and He would have saved her and restored her dignity. But she didn't because she didn't think that God could, or would, help her.

Not everyone is made for the same job. You cannot make yourself do something that you were not made to do. But God has a perfect job for you to do. This is what God will do: He will take someone who's been failing all of his or her life, someone who amounts to nothing, someone who's been laughed at, even put down and abused. He will take that person and lift him or her up.

In the same way, He will take you and lift you up. When everyone has lost hope in you, tossed you away, given up on you, God will take you up and make you a winner. He will make you victorious.

I know your situation; I know how you feel. I've been there; I've walked in your shoes. You may be weak, sickly, and pale; maybe fear has been eating at you. Maybe you feel lost, like death. Maybe the sun is shining, but you've surrendered to darkness.

Don't stay that way another minute! If you don't do something about it right now, you will die. Get up from the couch, lift up your chin, stand up tall, and tell yourself that you are not going to put up with this anymore. Let me tell you one more story because I want you to have a little hope. And hope will bring you strength.

Chapter 5

Power of God Verses Evil

Some years ago, I had a little condo on the third floor. I lived there for five years, long enough to get to know everyone in the complex. My girlfriend was visiting me one day when, all of a sudden, we heard a loud noise from below. We went to investigate and found a young man knocking on the door of a unit below. I asked him what was happening, and he replied that he was from AA, that the boy in this unit had called him on the phone and told him that he had had enough: He was going to kill himself.

We immediately called the police. The police arrived and began knocking on the door to no response. Just as they were about to break the door down, it opened, and a young man emerged. When he saw the police, he turned around and put his hands behind his back, as if he was ready to be cuffed. The cops told him, "We aren't here to arrest you; we want to help you."

I felt completely devastated. I didn't know much about the effects of alcohol and drugs on the human body so I was shocked by what I saw. How was it possible that this young man with his entire future ahead of him was so weak and helpless? He had tried to quit but had not been able to. He was rotting away, screaming for help, but everyone around him was helpless. I knew what I was seeing was a life from the pit of hell. Tears came to my eyes; I could not believe the waste. I knew that evil had no power, but why, then, were innocent children dying? How was it possible? I went over to him, took him into my arms and whispered words of encouragement, "Don't worry; everything will be okay." Then I went home as the police took care of him that night. But I could not sleep, thinking all night long about that troubled young man.

In the morning, I knocked on his door; he opened it and asked me in. I talked to him about Adam and Eve, about their sin and our curse, about God's plan for redemption. I told him about the good news, about the second chance, about freedom. He listened to me and said, "Look, I have a Bible, and I read it all the time." I asked him, "Do you understand the Bible?" "Just bits of it," he replied. I told him that he could be a child of the king, not a king of this world, but the King of Kings and Lord of Lords. We prayed together, and he asked God to be his Father.

A few weeks later, I saw him at the pool. He looked healthy and happy and said that he wasn't doing destructive things anymore. He was going to school, and his father was giving him a furnished condo. Things seemed to have turned around for him in a big way. I gave him a hug and told him how happy I was for him. When I got home, I cried with happiness. I had witnessed a miracle, right in front of my eyes. I had seen the power of God winning over evil. I had seen the mercy, compassion, and love of God winning over the lies, manipulation, and cruelty of Satan. I had seen God real and alive and right here in my own small neighborhood, performing His plan and saving His children from the cloves of Satan.

This story shows two extremes at work in our world: the power of good and the power of evil. Are they real? Yes, they are. They are even more real because they are powers in the spirit. Say that you get a cut in your body and it bleeds so you go to the hospital and get the wound stitched up. If you are wounded in your heart and your mind, however, no one can help you—except through the Spirit of mercy and love of God. How are you going to fight this evil? You can't fight with flesh and blood; you have to fight in the Spirit. Spirit of God is the only One that can help you.

Sins

Satan has only one purpose on this earth, to make you sin. When you sin, you destroy yourself. When you are with God, you will be healed in your mind, and then you will be healed in your body. Your mind, body, spirit, and soul become clear, peaceful, still, and complete. Some men brought to Jesus a paralyzed man, lying on a mat. When Jesus saw their faith, he said to the paralyzed man, "Take heart, son; your sins are forgiven." The people were so astonished and said, "How can anybody set you free from your sins?" But Jesus said, "Which is easier: to say, 'Your sins are forgiven,' or to say, 'Get up and walk'? But so that you may know that the Son of Man has authority on earth to forgive sins ..." Then he said to the paralyzed man, "Get up, take your mat, and go home," and he did.

There are two types of sin. The first is sin that you carry with you from your past. I call it "the addictive sin." The other is sin committed by your own choice, sin that you can choose to take or leave.

The addictive sin is the one that you need God to help you with. This is the sin that only God can remove. The other kind of sin is the sin of opportunity in your everyday life. For instance, you have the opportunity to steal something without anyone knowing about it. You have a choice whether to reject the opportunity or give in to it.

There is one thing common to all sins, and that is their outcome. God said that the result of sin is death. Sin poisons your body, spirit, and soul. Sin produces shame, sickness, depression, unworthiness, and ugliness. Sin separates you from your God, your happiness, and your joy. When you sin, guilt eats you up slowly, one piece at a time. You are alive, but you feel like death.

If there is a sin that you cannot give up, God will help you with it. Put your eyes on the Creator and Finisher of your faith. Don't let the addictive sin eat you up. Keep your eyes on God, and let Him help you.

God said, "Don't sin, but if you do, come to me, and I will help you." If you want to live in peace, health, joy, with a clear mind and conscience—then don't sin. Make a right choice. But when you do sin, ask God to help you. If you've asked God to help you already, you've tried to quit and you have failed, don't give up. Help is on the way.

Then there is the other sin—the sin that you freely choose—and this sin is another story. If you choose this sin and give in, you'll pay a big price for it.

Let's just say you have an opportunity for adultery. The adultery is staring you right in the face. It might even be constantly going after you, luring you, and hypnotizing you. Before you know it, you're involved and in danger of losing your family, your position, maybe your job. You feel guilty, ashamed, and maybe destructive.

Once a friend of mine had this choice to make, and she asked me what to do. I counseled her against it. But she said, "Oh, come on. What's going to happen? It's too exciting." And she decided to go for it. Some time passed, but then she had to deal with the results of her choice. I went to see her, and she was curled up on the floor, whimpering like a wounded animal begging for help. I wanted to help her, but I was not able. Oh yes, she got over it and straightened up her life, but it took her five years. And the damage to her relationships had been done.

People ask me what my worst sin was. Sin is as individual as the person: One person has a problem with hate, another with pornography, another with adultery. My worst sin could mean nothing to you, and maybe your worst sin would be unthinkable to me. Sin is sin, and whatever you are struggling with is your own worst nightmare. God said that He will set us free from all our sins, and we will not be prisoners of sin anymore.

Sin will always bring pain, not only to your own life, body, and mind but also to the lives of those around you. If you have a choice to get involved with sin and you don't care about the results the sin will bring into your life, think about your loved ones. Don't destroy them, especially children. They don't deserve it.

I see it all the time: Parents get divorced, but the children have to live with the consequences. Parents go on to rebuild their lives, but the children never recover. God put these children into the parents' hands to care for, but instead, they are slowly damaging them. The children travel from one household to the other, they don't have stability, and they can't concentrate. They look on as their parents change partners all the time. What is going through their heads? Is it any wonder why these children struggle, why they are on drugs, why they don't have confidence or self-respect? They don't even know what is right and what is wrong because they have been shown the wrong example. Sometimes they are blamed for destroying their parents' lives. In truth, it is the children's lives that have been hurt.

I am concerned about what is going on right here, in our homeland. The biggest trick of the enemy is to confuse us so much that we destroy ourselves. This is the cleverest kind of manipulation. You can worry about the war; you can worry about terrorism, but look into your own house, and what do you see? Do you see frightened and neglected children? Do you see women afraid of their own husbands? Do you see children being sold for pornography? Or seduced by drugs? I tell you, my friend, that we are creating our own kind of terrorism, right here in our own back yard.

Let's say that you lived through the age of drugs in your youth and it didn't really affect you. Your life is going just fine. But what if a child in your family was on drugs? Would you give this young person an ultimatum—stop or you will have to leave the house and the family? I didn't have any problems, and you shouldn't either.

Would you please think about this child with me for a second? Maybe you were lucky; maybe when hard drugs came around, you were already grown up. Maybe you were just smart enough or old enough to understand what this thing could do to you. But don't think that, because it was easy for you to avoid dependency, it is equally easy for your child. You must have compassion and understanding for the youth of this day and age.

Kids today face a lot of challenges and pressures. Some of them are from broken homes, some have lived with poverty, hunger, or abuse, some are scared, and some are just insecure and vulnerable to all kinds of peer pressure. Someone older and smarter can use the innocence and naïveté of children to introduce them to drugs. If they get hooked, they enter a world of lying, stealing, and desperation. Often these kids travel in packs. Some may call them gangs, rebels, hooligans, but I call them lost, used, broken, and wounded.

They are young and naïve; they believed, and that was their crime. Now they are hooked and don't know how to stop. What they need is you, your love, and your help. Don't push them away. Now it is your turn: You have to do something. You cannot put your hands down; you cannot give up on your children. When you are feeling frightened about terrorism, suicide bombs, and war, please take a look at your children. We are already in a war if they are not safe from every danger.

Likewise, I see people around me offending one another all the time. And it breaks my heart. God is a shield and protector of innocents and babes. There are only a few woes—sins that truly merit God's judgment—in God's law, but if you ignore them, the punishment is severe.

God wants us to be free; this is the most important part of God's plan for us. Everything that God has done for us so far is leading to our freedom. If someone works deliberately against God's plan, God will deal with him very severely. God said, "Woe to the world because of offense. Such things must come, but woe to the man through whom they come." God's woe means that if you ignore this part of God's law it would be better for you to have a large millstone hung around your neck and to be drowned in the depths of the sea.

Next time when you think to offend people, to make them sin, to put them down, to make them fall, to make them little, to use them or take advantage of their innocence, especially that of a child, you'd better think about it twice. Soon afterwards, you might feel as if you are drowning, and you will wonder why. Woe be unto you.

Weapons of the Warfare

We worry about war and about the atomic bomb. Oh yes, the possibilities are catastrophic. Let's follow God's strategy first. God says, "For we wrestle not against flesh and blood, but against principalities, against powers, against the rulers of the darkness of this world, against spiritual wickedness in high places. Therefore, take into you the whole armor of God that you may be able to withstand the evil day, and having done so, to stand.

"Stand, therefore, with your loins girded about with truth, the breastplate of righteousness about you, your feet shod with the protection of the gospel of peace. Take the shield of faith in hand, wherewith you shall be able to quench all the fiery darts of the wicked. Take the helmet of salvation and the sword of the Spirit, praying always with supplication in the Spirit and watching with perseverance for the supplication of all saints."

God gave us spiritual weapons to fight spiritual wickedness. Through the Spirit of God, those weapons are available to every child of God. Until now, you've been a being of this world, under the control of evil, and unable to stand against evil attacks. You were not able to fight. When you were hurt, you didn't know any better so you blamed each other. The enemy makes you believe that you should blame someone else and, therefore, sets you against each other. The result is much anger, bitterness, and hate.

Now you have the armor of God. Now you can go to war against evil because the armor of God is your defense. Let's try to understand what the biblical verse above is telling us.

Loins girded about with truth—Your loins are a region of strength in your body. Truth is like your loins; it will give you strength.

The breastplate of righteousness about you—Righteousness is the breastplate over your heart; because you are righteous through the blood of Jesus, sin has no power over you.

Your feet shod with the protection of the gospel of peace—The gospel of peace keeps your feet from stumbling and falling while you are walking through life.

The shield of faith—Faith is like a shield that protects you from enemy attacks; if you have faith, arrows will not pierce you.

The helmet of salvation—Salvation is like a helmet that protects evil thoughts from coming into your mind.

The sword of the spirit—Spirit of God is like a sword, and this is the only one weapon that you maneuver or need. Everything else is armor, a protection from the enemy, but the sword is something that you kill with. If the enemy attacks you, you kill him with a sword, with the Spirit of God.

You may say—*Are you telling me that we are walking around with this armor?* Yes, the whole body is protected with armor. It is invisible armor. If you know the world of God and you know His Spirit, you are not only protected but you also will defeat the enemy.

When the enemy comes to thwart you with his tricks and lies, you are not going to listen, and you will not be afraid. Because you know the truth and you know his tricks, you'll recognize him right away. This knowledge will give you confidence and strength, but above all, you will have the Spirit of God always right next to you, fighting for you.

How is this going to happen? Now that you have the Spirit of God in you, every step that you take is like walking with an invisible bodyguard. Before, everything in you was working towards the worst; now everything in you will be working towards the better and the best, with the protection of God's Spiritual weapons.

Have you ever seen a little boy with his little fists stretched out towards you, trying to fight with you? Isn't this just funny? You put your hand on his head, and he kicks and screams, and you are just having fun with him. It's the same thing with evil. If you have the Spirit of God in you, evil can only be like that little boy, flailing away but ineffectual.

Chapter 6

The Fruits of the Spirit and Fruits of This World

If you walk by the law of the Spirit, you will reap the fruits of the Spirit. If you walk by the law of this world, you will reap the fruits of this world.

The fruits of the Spirit are love, joy, peace, righteousness and truth, patience, gentleness, goodness, faith, meekness, temperance. Against such, there is no law. The fruits of this world are immorality, impurity, indecency, idolatry, sorcery, enmity, strife, jealousy, anger, selfishness, divisions, envy, drunkenness, carousing, and the like.

God said that we should walk by the Spirit. The results will always be the fruits of the Spirit. If you walk by the Spirit, you will not produce any destruction, and no one will ever be hurt; the results will always be good and positive for you and others.

Right at the moment that you decide to follow the Spirit of God and live in peace and joy, the way of this world is going to be standing right next to you. The voice will be telling you to go the shallow way, using formulas and methods. Please don't be fooled. You can have wonderful ideas and something exiting to do in your life, but if you use the way of this world to get it, it is going to end up feeling as shallow and meaningless as the way you obtained it.

To walk by the Spirit is like sculpting the granite body of Michelangelo's *David*. The results are permanent—beautiful forever. Do you want to create something that no one bothers to take notice of? Or you do you want to create another *Mona Lisa* or *David*—something noble and unforgettable? Use the way of God's Spirit to get it, and you will produce a masterpiece.

Throughout the ages, people have tried to create systems of law that fit their needs and wants, but they have never really gotten it right. I've heard people ask: How do you know if this is right or this is wrong? You will know the difference by the fruits you are reaping, by the results of your actions. If you follow the Spirit, you will always feel peaceful, content, and joyful.

Anytime you feel angry, uneasy, or confused—pay attention because those feelings are trying to tell you that something is not right, that you are doing something wrong, or that you have put yourself in the wrong situation. As soon as those feelings come, you need to find the cause of those feelings and try to correct the situation right away or get this situation out of your life. You can't force anything on your body. Poison will always be poison, whether it's in your body or your spirit. If you keep your body in this state of stress, you will surely make it sick.

Over and over again, I see people get themselves into dangerous or destructive situations that they could have avoided. You need to be very careful about your choices, not only because you might hurt someone but also because you will reap whatever you sow.

My girlfriend called me late one night. She was angry and hyperventilating. "You've got to come over. I'm ready to buy a car, and I'm very confused. It's getting late, and they're about to close up the place. You have to help me." I asked her, "Why don't you buy it tomorrow?" But she replied, "Oh no, I need to buy it now because they might sell it before I can get there tomorrow. I am just so confused." I said, "You are confused and under pressure; the only thing for you to do is get out from this situation right away and go home. You can always come back tomorrow." But she insisted she had to buy it now. So I told her, "I won't be able to help you. It looks as if you've made up your mind already anyway." She bought the car and had a problem with it for many, many years.

If you would only pay more attention to your spirit, there are so many warnings and so many signs. You might be running around, consulting psychologists or psychics, but you don't realize that the answer is right here under your nose.

A woman friend of mine was going on her first date with a new fellow she had just met. After the date, she called me up to give me her report: "We had a great time. He is very good looking, and he's a doctor." Just as I was thinking that he could be the one, she added, "But …" At that moment, I knew something was wrong. Adding "but" to your sentence is a telltale indication that something is wrong. I said, "You'd better take a second look at this fellow; he could be trouble." She told me I was imagining things, and our conversation came to an end. She had another date with him, and this time when she called, she was devastated. Again, he had been very nice at dinner, but he had ended up leaving her without paying the bill. Her original "but" had turned out to be warranted.

Many times, common sense will tell you what is the right and what is the wrong choice. But many other times, people find themselves in unique situations where simple common sense can't help them. When you come across a difficult choice and you have no idea what to do, at that moment, you need the Spirit of God the most.

God says, "Be still and know that I am God." What does this mean? This means God knows that when we are under pressure and we are not able to make a good and sound decision, we have to learn how to be patient and turn to Him.

When you are in a very difficult situation, it often seems as if there is no way out. When you know that you have done everything possible and the situation has not changed, don't panic. At a moment like this, God is telling you, "I have control over this situation, and you have to let me do it." At a moment like this, you have to stop. You have to let it go, and you have to wait. I have good news for you, my friend; the miracle is around the corner.

God wants to help you, to give you good direction, and sometimes He wants His glory to be seen. That means He wants to lift you up and exalt you in someone's eyes.

To illustrate what I mean, I will tell you a story. I was working for a big manufacturing company, and I had a responsible position there. My supervisor started to look for reasons to humiliate me, never mind why. Every day, I would come to work, and there was a new situation that made me feel stressful, confused, and humiliated.

In the beginning, I defended myself, but instead of helping, it drove me deeper into the hole. I was becoming physically sick. The situation was getting so out of hand that I hated to go to work. One day, I was so afraid to go to work that my whole body shook like a leaf. I got on the floor, on my hands and knees, and I cried, "Please God, help me. Don't send me there anymore. They step all over my dignity; they chew me up and spit me out." After praying for a little while, I heard the quiet little voice, and peace came over me—*Let it go; leave it alone. Let Me do it.*

I put on my clothes and went to work. From that time on, I didn't pay any attention to what was going on around me. I was at peace, and peace was getting me through it. I did not defend myself anymore, and I did not care what people were thinking about me. Meanwhile, my supervisor was ruining my reputation and trying to lay me off. But

I was a very good worker, and they could not fire me. To make a long story short, the day came for me to leave the company. I went to my supervisor's office and said, "I have come to say goodbye. I am very sorry for offending you; forgive me for whatever it was that I said or did." He took his glasses off and for a moment was silent. Then he said, "I am sorry you are leaving the company. You have been a light in this department, and we will miss you. Please keep in touch."

After a couple of months, I got an offer for a new job. The company needed references from my old supervisor, so I had to give them his number. He must have said something good about me because I got the job. And getting it was the best thing to happen to me. I stepped onto a new road in my life, a road that led me to a new dimension and new opportunities. I saw God in a new light. I had trusted Him, and in return, He had given me something beyond my imagination, something I couldn't conceive on my own. This was the beginning of my new life, together with my God.

A few months later, the company that laid me off started losing orders and had to lay off thousands of people. The future of this company continues to be very shaky. My supervisor wanted to destroy me, but actually, he saved me from disaster.

God wants to help you, but most of all He wants you to see who He is so you can trust Him. The more you trust Him, the more He can bring you into a new dimension, into new and marvelous things. He said, "Try me, if I will not open for you the windows of heaven and pour you out a blessing that there shall not be room enough to receive it."

Trust in God. Then one day, you will get up in the morning, you will open up your eyes, and everything will look different to you. Oh, yes, you will still see trees and houses and people. But you will see them in a different dimension because you will know without doubt that behind everything you see there is something beautiful waiting for you every day.

When you come to this point in your life, you will understand why you cannot compromise, why you need always to choose the best.

Compromise

Yes, you will want to go fast and not waste your time. You will notice rationalizations coming up in your mind. "You are getting older," the voice will say. "The time for childbearing will soon pass you by." Or the voice will say, "Look at yourself; you're getting older. Who is going to take care of you?" Or maybe this: "When you are going to have some fun? Life is passing you by." And so on and so on.

I tell you, if you listen to these voices and compromise, you will never know your true destiny. You'll be chasing the wind; you will never be satisfied, and no matter what you accomplish, it is going to be a waste.

A woman marrying a man for his money, a student choosing a profession he doesn't like because it seems lucrative, a businessman compromising his integrity to get a client, a girl working in a strip club to make some easy money…what will happen to these people? They are slowly dying inside, and they will not stop dying until, one day, they get up in the morning and want to shoot themselves.

Do you feel depressed, suicidal, with no reason to live? Please, do me a favor. Look inside yourself; be honest and tell me, where did you compromise? Who took advantage of you? Who used you? Did you give yourself away to someone and now you feel as if you sold your soul? I am so sorry if this is you. I want to take you in my arms and tell you that it is not too late. You can turn it all around; you can change this situation. You are not an insect crawling around in the dust. In reality, you are a noble creature—a child of God.

Maybe you say—*But you don't understand; it's too late for me. I cannot change anything about myself or about my life. I try to protect myself and run away from change. I can't do it; I'm very weak, lazy, a complainer.*

Okay, I can see where you going with this. I need to tell you about people in the kingdom of this world so you can understand. And when you understand, you will know the truth, and the truth will set you free.

There are three types of people in this world: givers, takers, and the free people. All of them want to take something from this world. But the way they choose to take it makes a big difference.

Givers will give you everything they have to get from you what they want. Takers will do the opposite: they will use force to take from you whatever they want. It is very interesting to observe them and the way they accomplish their goals. They have all kinds of methods and plans to achieve them. Most of them don't even realize what they are doing. If you tell them about the methods they are using, they are shocked and offended. They have been getting everything they want for so long they don't even realize how they are doing it.

We should not be shocked. We've lived in this world for many thousands of years, and we've been learning from each other all that time. Over many generations, we've learned all sorts of poisonous behaviors and passed them along to our children. When those children grow up, they use the manipulating games of the giver or the taker throughout their entire lives without giving them a thought.

There are many everyday examples of manipulation at work. A child throws a tantrum so he can pressure his mother into buying him a toy; a young woman uses her looks and wiles to get a rich husband; a man pledges his love to get a woman into his bed. Sales and business people have their tried-and-true methods for making the sale, signing the deal. And thieves, terrorists, and murderers have theirs, including extortion, violence, and fear. You can go into the bookstore and pick up a number of different titles devoted to strategies for getting almost anything you want. Then you can use cruel games to go after it. When you get what you want, you expect to be happy, and when you aren't, you can go back to the bookstore for another volume on achieving happiness and peace. But no book, including this one, will bring you the happiness and peace you seek unless you change your motives.

I see it like this: Say you're a man who's been hurt in his marriage, and you've promised yourself that it won't happen again. But you have your needs and want a woman. So what's your move now? If you get involved with a woman again, you'll get hurt. So you lie and manipulate someone into intimacy with you without engaging your own emotions. And why shouldn't you? Hasn't someone done the same to you?

After a little while, you feel depressed, shameful, and guilty so you try to figure out what's wrong with you. You go to the doctor, get some medication, and you think you're going to be okay. But in fact, you are rotting away inside. If you continue like this, one day, you will have no feelings left.

You may say—*So who cares?* Well, you should, for one. You should care because you'll end up with no feelings, which impacts not only your emotional life but also your ability to make choices, decisions, and judgments in your life. Ultimately, it affects your ability to be someone and to get somewhere. Everyone wants to be somebody; everyone wants to win. But some of us are doing the wrong things to get there.

There's a reason we are this way and do the wrong things. Sometime, somehow, someone tried to get something from us through manipulation. We were taken advantage of and got hurt. Now we're paralyzed and don't know what to do. We've been messed up and deceived. We've been lied to and hypnotized and now we need to find out what has been stolen from us, what we have lost.

I want to tell you that behind all your games and manipulations there is someone very special. Think for a minute. Does your life depend on learning how to manipulate people and circumstances? Or does it depend on finding out who you really are? Take a good look at yourself in the mirror. Look at yourself and say: *I've got to stop; I've got to remove myself from this cycle of repeating madness. I've got to start thinking in a new way.*

You must come to the realization that your life is much more than things and games. Your life is who you are inside, in your spirit; it's what you think, what makes you happy. Your life is about discovering new dreams and achieving them, not by hurting someone else on the way to a fleeting triumph. You don't want to be either a giver or a taker; you really long to be the third type of person. You want to be free.

To Be Free

What is it like to be free? I am talking about a person who has no past pains and no past wounds. Yes, this person has memories. He was born to this world so he has been hurt just like you and me. But he was transformed, he arrived, he won. What is the most significant thing about this free person?

He lives in this world, but he does not belong to this world. He does not move by the law of this world; he moves by the law of the Spirit of God. He lives for the Spirit of God, and he moves by it. And the Spirit always wins.

Nothing in this world can hurt him. He lives here, but he is not attached to this world because he has overcome the world. He and the Father are one. Who can stand against him? Who can hurt him? What can people do to him? The evil of this world has no hold on him. But he understands pain, confusion, and fear because he's experienced it. He knows how much people hurt in this world.

He believes in dignity and freedom for all and fights for it. He is not afraid, so he fights for the innocent, for the babes. He has the weapons of the warfare so he moves with confidence. He has the power to move mountains because he knows the trick of the enemy. He has the keys to the kingdom of heaven; whatever he opens on earth is opened in heaven, and whatever he closes is closed in heaven.

He sees the people of this world as confused, without purpose, like birds with broken wings. He empathizes with them; he wants to help them and tell them the truth. The days do not run away from him anymore; rather, every day is a new discovery and a new adventure. He feels that time has stopped for him, and he looks forward to every day with excitement and anticipation. He has a passion;

it is his gift from God, the very purpose that he was born for. The passion is burning in him as a fire and consuming his very being.

To be free; this is the most important part of God's law. Everything that God has done for us so far is leading to our freedom. The only time we can give truth and pure love is when we are free. The only way we can love God is when we are free.

Curse and Blessing

You may say—*This free person that you are talking about could not come from the same past that I have because he could not have changed that much. He could not have let all of that go.*

You need to understand that after Adam and Eve sinned, everything became cursed. From that time on, everything they or their progeny did was cursed; even the ground they walked and worked on was cursed. In Deuteronomy, God said that if you were cursed, no matter what you did and how hard you worked, nothing would flourish and multiply. In other words, you work hard but get very little out of your work. The harvest from your hard work will be very poor.

On the other hand, if you are blessed, you are in the opposite situation. Everything you do with a minimum of effort will flourish and multiply. Everything that you touch will turn to gold. God said that He would open the windows of heaven and pour blessing upon you, so much that you will not be able to contain it.

Have you ever asked yourself—Why do I make the same mistake over and over again? No matter how much you try to fix your mistake, you do it the same way the next time and get yourself into the same old problems.

You are repeating the same old mistakes, working with the same old patterns, because you are under the curse and your past drives you to do the same things over and over again. Every time you make a move, you make it the same way. You are on automatic—you push the button, and the same things come up.

You need to be blessed. And to be blessed, you need the Spirit of God. When you are blessed and not cursed, everything works for you, not against you. Together with your blessing, you are learning a new way of living, and this is making you a new person, totally different from before.

This part of the Bible rejuvenated me. For a while, I was convinced that somebody had cursed me. After all my hard work and all my misfortune, I was looking to blame somebody for my unfortunate life. While visiting my parents, I asked them to pray for me and bless me because I thought prayer would break my curse. Then I learned that all of us are under the curse.

When you are transformed, you will start making better decisions and get better results. You will be surprised at how your life has become totally different from before. When you encounter a situation that totally defeated you in the past, you will find yourself a winner in the same situation. No one will dare to hurt you or put you down. No one will point fingers at you or take advantage of you. You will not be afraid but will look for opportunities to try new things and challenges. You will be proud of yourself, and the world will look different to you. God said that the day would come when His children would be free from bondage and slavery. You are not going to be a slave to anybody or anything anymore. You are going to be a winner.

When you find out who you are, your sense of your own value will go sky high. You will start watching every choice you make, and you will stop compromising. You will stop looking on your life as inconsequential and realize that every day has value and purpose.

You are part of a puzzle, one little piece, but if you look from afar, you will see the big picture. You will see that you are here not just for your lifetime, a span of seventy or eighty years. The real thing is not here on earth; you are just passing through. The real thing is your life together with God for eternities to come. When you see your life this way, you are going to realize that your life is very valuable, and you will take every day as a gift from God.

Every day, you will get up and embrace the whole of it—both the good and the bad. The fact is, you don't always know what is good for you and what is bad. Sometimes a situation that looks painful is just the bridge to something wonderful. Instead of panicking and blaming someone, just let it happen; something beautiful may come up. God will help you through it, and you will be a better person for it

Every day that you get up in the morning, you will embrace it as a gift from God. You will realize that every moment has a purpose and a connection, one with another. You have to remember that when God starts with you, He will not stop but will take you through to the end. Without God, life is so meaningless.

But, not all of us are going to be transformed; not all of us are going to be free. God said that there would be a time when people come to Him like a flood and they will be as water covering the earth. Think of the analogy: three-quarters of the earth is covered with water; perhaps three-quarters of the world's people will flock to God. But what will happen with the others? Those souls will choose evil over God.

God has put two doors in front of us: the door to life and the door to death. There will be a time when everyone has a chance to test and to see that God is good. Those who choose God will be free and live in peace. It is hard to believe that after all the teaching and all the promises from God, there are still going to be people who will choose evil. But we already see this in our world: people who choose brutality and violence, people who seem to enjoy evil and the power it brings, people who love chaos and garbage and feed on it like rats.

Prayer

You are praying whenever you call on the name of God or communicate with Him in any way or form. Why do you need to do this? You go to the throne of God because you need His power, His strength, His wisdom, His love, and His mercy. Right here at His footstool, you gain the ability to fight evil in this world and to become a winner.

As soon as you receive the Spirit from God, you have access to all of God's privileges. Even if there is still work to be done in you, immediately, you have a right to everything God has for you. You are able to go to God and communicate with him, you are able to seek his advice, and as often as you sin, you are able to go to God and ask Him to make you pure and clean. As soon as you become His child, God sees you as pure and clean, perfect in His eyes.

You ask—*How can this be?* You are still impure, you are still full of shame and fear, you are still sinning, and God is treating you as a perfect, righteous person? Isn't He angry? Isn't He furious?

No, God is not angry. He knows where you are coming from, and He knows where you are going. He knows that you need to be transformed, but this does not stop Him from loving you and spending time with you right away. God is your loving Father.

The loving mother and father do not reject their child because she makes a mistake. The parents know that the child needs to learn about life, and if she makes mistakes, this is an indication that she doesn't know what to do, that she still has learning to do. After the child's mistake, her parents continue to love her, care for her, and teach her the correct way to behave. And that's the way it is for the children of God.

So you go to God, and you pray. The first thing you need to do is ask God to cleanse you from your sins with the blood of Jesus Christ because you need to be clean, righteous, and pure when you go to the throne of God. You need to go with confidence. The Bible says, "Come boldly to the throne of God." You have a right to go to God, and you have a right to ask for everything you need. You know that everything has been done for you and you are on your way to freedom. But before you get there, God will give you protection from your enemy: the protection of the blood of Jesus, the protection of prayer, and the weapons of the warfare.

After you sin, there will be guilt, which will keep you away from God. Guilt will tell you that you are no good, not worthy to be a child of God. This is why you need to get clean as often as possible, so the enemy cannot throw guilt in your face and use it against you. Ask God for forgiveness from your sin, and the blood of Jesus will clean you and free you from guilt and shame, just as if it had never happened. If you need to make something right with someone you have hurt, God will inspire you to ask the person's forgiveness.

Because you are not yet familiar with God's ways, in the beginning, you might ask God for things that are not good for you. God will always direct you towards the best for you. Sometimes you will not understand what is best for you, sometimes it will take more time for the best to become manifest in your life. The most important thing to know is that the fastest way to God is to trust Him completely.

Please, be patient. God is working in you; give Him a chance to transform you into His image. The worst thing you can think is that God doesn't care about you or doesn't love you. Don't be fooled by the enemy—he comes to lie, steal, and destroy your life in God.

Talk with God, tell him about your pains, tell him your problems and worries, and by all means, ask Him for anything you need. If you don't understand what is going on in your life, ask Him to explain it to you. I communicate with God best by writing things down, by talking to Him on paper. I have been writing letters to my lover—God—for twenty years.

Every time I start writing to God, I know only that I need Him. Then I open up my heart, tell Him all my problems, and know that He will always show me understanding. He puts me at ease and on the right path. I have boxes and boxes of letters to my God, and each one is a homage to His love, His compassion, His mercy, His wonders, His miracles, His wisdom, and above all, His majesty.

He is every breath I take. He is every particle of blood that flows through my veins. He is my All in all, my every answer, and my every joy because, you see, I don't live anymore but my God lives in me. I am His and He is mine. He is my hands, and He is my eyes.

I stand in front of His throne, bowed low to the ground, giving Him honor and glory, not because He is worthy to be praised but because He is my King of Kings and my Lord of Lords. Everything that I am belongs to Him.

Chapter 7

God's Final Plan

God has everything in control. After the sin, the world became cursed, confused, and out of control, but God has a plan. He is protecting and preserving His plan. Nothing is going to happen in this world without God, no war and no disaster. God has said that He will not stop until He has done what He plans to do.

First, God is building His army, and His army will cover the whole earth. God is going to take back from Satan what was stolen from Him. But nothing is going to happen on this earth until God is ready to move. There are going to be wars and rumors of the war, but you need not worry. Have peace; the time for the big war is not yet here. God is not going to start His victory with a weak and fearful army. To do His work, God needs an army of heroes, an army with strength, an army with God's vision.

If you choose to be with God, you are going to be a candidate for a soldier in His army, just as right now, God is working on those that are already with Him. His army will be filled with strength, power, and confidence. It is going to be so strong that it will rise up in the name of Jesus and make things happen.

The power of God will give you strength and help you do things that you were not able to do before. It will be like magic. God's knowledge will be so clear and so will be your understanding that nothing will stand in your way. You will destroy all opposition; you will kick open every door. You will have vision and purpose, you will know how to fight, and you will not be afraid. When you come to this point with God, you will know without doubt that God is real, that He has a plan for his people.

People ask me—*Why do I need to wait on God and do what He tells me to do?* If you want to go the better and the higher way—the way of the Kingdom of God—it is going to be very important that you work together with God. He will reveal to you what He is doing, but you will not know His time or His way of accomplishing it.

If you go ahead on your own, you will mess everything up. God could have been preparing you for this assignment all of your life. When He reveals this assignment to you, you will be excited. But if you persist in doing things your own way, you will lose your vision, and the plan that you were made for will be wasted.

Revelation

Many people have tried to understand the last book of the Bible—the Book of Revelation. They have tried to explain the meaning of it, but the words in Revelation are hidden for now, hidden from this world and from God's children. Why? I don't know, and I am not trying to figure it out. I can only understand the first part in Revelation, and this is enough for me.

The first part in Revelation is very clear. Jesus will break the first seal from the scroll. The scroll is a book of things to come: God's final plan to conquer the earth and save His creation from Satan. Jesus will be riding on a white horse with a bow in his hand. The white horse is not a warhorse but represents purity and righteousness. Jesus's victory is so sure that He is going to ride as a victorious king on a white horse to overtake the enemy.

The bow in Jesus's hand is His strength; His sharp arrows are God's words, and they always hit their mark. Christ is a king, and He will be wearing a crown. The kingdom of Christ will be established and enlarged in spite of all opposition. If you receive Jesus as your savior, then you must be loyal and obedient to Him. Everything that God does, He does with precise detail. Nothing ever is wasted, and nothing is done without purpose.

Because of the opposition, His work will not be done in a short time. Before Jesus goes forth and conquers the earth, people will be going to God like a flood. They will cover the earth like water. At that time, every tongue and every breath will be saying the name of the Lord. The next thing on God's agenda will be to collect His children, riding upon the white horse.

When the second seal is broken, the red horse, the horse of war, will appear. People that have stayed behind and refused Jesus's salvation will be witness to the war of judgment. I don't want to scare you, but the time is coming for things on this earth to become firm and decisive.

If someone came to your house and took your priceless, dearest, most valuable thing away from you, would you just sit there and let him have it? Would you not start planning to retrieve it and never stop thinking about your plan until you'd gotten back your treasure? Neither will God. God has a plan to claim His children, and when He is ready, He will fulfill it—with you or without you.

You may think that now is the time for war and the earth's destruction, but I tell you that nothing will happen until God's plan is fulfilled.

Chapter 8

Citizens of the Kingdom of God

God said, "I will put My law in their inward parts and write it in their hearts; and I will be their God, and they shall be My people." There is a time in your life with God when you will come to the end of your journey. All the searching and all the pain will finally be transformed into peace and contentment, and you will be a new, free, and complete person.

To get there, we need to make a decision, a decision to redeem what was stolen from us and to accept that we were cheated, lied to, misled, and manipulated. Without a fight and without resistance, we accepted blows from our enemy. For centuries, we lived with limited resources, and we did nothing about it.

So, we ask you, Father, to forgive us. Forgive us for being content without a gift of life from God to His children.

Forgive us for being ignorant, for accepting things of this world without exploring possibility.

We didn't understand. Satan stepped over us and ruled over us. We hurt, and we suffered, and we didn't care. Our Father, we pray, "Give us a chance for a new beginning, give us a chance to regain our dignity, and give us a strength and confidence to fight for what is ours. In the name of Jesus Christ, we pray."

Get on your knees with me; you are in front of the throne of God. Say it out loud—"My Heavenly Father, I come to you by my own choice, and I ask You to forgive me for my sins. I understand that Jesus died on the cross for my sins and He opened the door for me to become Your child again. Take me back, please. Make me clean and pure; wash away all my sins, all my shame, all my poisons, all my pain and wounds with the blood of Jesus. Teach me Your law and Your way. Bring me back to Your kingdom. Amen, in the name of Jesus."

After you pray this prayer, find yourself a church, buy yourself a Bible, and start reading from the New Testament. You are about to reclaim your inheritance and begin your new life as a beloved child of God. And there is nothing more thrilling than the turn your life has now taken.

The Lord blesses you and keeps you. The Lord makes His face shine upon you and be gracious to you. The Lord turns His face towards you and gives you peace—the peace beyond all understanding.

Answer to the Question

The time is come to answer the question that I asked in the beginning of this book—Why are we here?

We are here, going through this life, and living on this earth and not in heaven with God to learn, to be perfected, and to be made in the image of God so that when we die we will go to live with God in heaven.

To be made in the image of God, we have to go down this road and learn the good and the evil and the results of each. This is the way God is. He knows the good and the evil, and He has a choice. He makes only good choices because He is wise and knows the results of good and evil choices. This is why He is perfect.

Adam and Eve were perfect when they were created. They could not live in heaven because they did not know good and evil. They did not know how to make choices. Then they made a bad choice, and they sinned.

All of these centuries after Adam and Eve, we have continued to learn about good and evil and how to live with them. It is taking us a long time because we have to find the right way, and if something doesn't work, we have to try again.

In the beginning after the fall, we tried to live by the law. The law brought rules and regulations, and we found that the law didn't work for us. We were still prisoners of our sins.

This world is pulling us into the wheel of deception. We spin around and around so quickly that we can't breathe, think, or react without fear, pain, and confusion. So we repeat our mistakes over and over again, losing ourselves in the process. We don't know that we can jump off this wheel of deception and walk into the stillness and reality of life by taking the gift that has been handed to us from our Father.

Then Jesus came and gave us the way to God. We thought that to go to God we needed to be good. So, we created our good character to please God. We knew that if we did "good," we would not go to hell. This way of living caused frustration in lots of people, and some of us gave up. Some of us thought that God was cruel and asking the impossible from us because we had tried and we could not be good.

God said, "Without faith, it is impossible to please me." How could we have missed this part of the Bible for so long? God is asking us for faith to trust Him, and after we trust Him, He will make us perfect.

Instead of trying to manufacture good character, we can receive attention from God by faith, just by trusting him. When we learn who God is, we trust Him, and then we will be able to lean on Him. We will not be worried; we will not fight or be suspicious of others.

While we are here on earth, we will continue to trust God, to go to Him and ask His forgiveness. In this way, we will continue to be made free and perfect each time we ask Him for it. Then Jesus will come and take us to heaven. We will be just like God and be able to live with Him in love, peace, and joy.

You may ask—*How we will live in heaven without a body?* I don't know, and I'm not worried about it. I know that God has a choice to live in a body on this earth or without a body in heaven. He chooses to live without a body in heaven. This tells me that, even if the earth were perfect, to live in heaven is better than on the earth. I want to be made in the image of God, and I want to live in heaven with Him.

Jesus lived on this earth in a human body. He died and went to hell. He could not stay there because He was perfect and without sin. The same is going to happen to you and me. If we live on this earth with God's Holy Spirit and learn the way of God, we will be made perfect with God's mercy and grace, and hell cannot hold us. We will go to heaven as Jesus did.

When I look on this world, I see the world as God saw it: Everything that He made was very good in His eyes, and He blessed it. Everything on earth was created in perfect harmony; it was created for a reason and with a purpose. Birds and animals are sheltered from sun and weather by trees and vegetation. Wind and animals spread the seeds, and rain waters the flowers, trees, fruits, and vegetables so we have food to eat. Water evaporates and comes back to earth cleansed so we have water to drink. And as God's children, we human beings are higher than the animals and very important to God's overall plan and purpose.

I am a piece of the big picture where God, my creator, is in control. So I go to Your throne, my God and my Father, to seek Your will, to be a vassal, to implement Your plan, and to draw on Your strength to follow Your plan through. "Your kingdom will come to this earth; your will be done on earth as it is in heaven." Amen.

Walking into New Life

I have learned how to live, and I will never run away from life again. I feel as if someone has come, opened up the windows of my life, and allowed a fresh breeze to sweep through my whole house. I have become new, fresh all over. All of a sudden, my body has straightened up tall, I've lifted my chin, and I am somebody. I am important. I belong to Somebody, and He loves me. I have the purpose and plan of my Father to carry forward. And I will be with Him for eternity.

My body, my soul, and my spirit have been healed, and I have been made whole. All of a sudden, I love life. I don't worry about my future anymore, and I don't worry about getting older. I don't think about making my dreams come true or making something of my life. I have a purpose and a reason, and I am going to be living it every day of my life. I am no longer afraid of sickness, pain, and loneliness. There is something stronger and bigger inside me, something that lifts me up above all the fears and horrors of this life. I've discovered I am living in this world but I am not of this world. This world has no hold on me. Now I know deep down in my spirit and my soul that, even if disaster strikes and knocks me to my knees, I won't crawl—I will fly. I am free.

My dream has come true. The words GO AND GET IT do not ring in my ears anymore. My God has fulfilled His promise. This whole world feels like a big field, open in front of me. And I feel like a little girl running into this field to pick up all the beautiful, shining, and glittering presents of this life that are lying there in wait for me.

What is there for me? I will find out. I will go and I will get it. I know that I am starting my life for the first time. I know that life has just begun for me. What will I do? How will I be? It does not matter because I know that whatever it is, it's going to be wonderful.

I took a chance on God and gambled in the biggest game ever. And I won. I stood behind the opened door. I looked at a bright shining light and knew that I was home. I had arrived, and the wide, open arms of my God were holding me, welcoming me. His love showered down upon me. Nothing was important to me anymore. He was mine, and I was His. We were together, and we were one. All the pains, wounds, struggles, disappointments, defeats, shames, and fears of my life have brought me here to this moment.

Were they worth it? YES. Every moment of my past life, every darkness, depression, and sickness has sculpted the new life I live today. I have lived through the good and through the evil, and the good has triumphed. I am a winner because of good. God was the Good, and He's proved to me that He was the Truth. I do not have to search anymore. What I have discovered completely overwhelms me.

I lifted my hands up to God to worship Him and to pray. To my surprise, the words coming from my mouth were not like my words of prayer to God before. I felt as if I was physically standing in front of God's throne and saying words of prayer to Him. The words coming from my mouth to my God were flowing—just as if they were alive.

I was kneeling on my bed in the darkness of the night, but I was not there; I was with Him in His throne room. It was not a vision, and it was not dream. It was my new reality, my new life, my new beginning.

For the first time in my life, I knew and understood what Jesus meant when He said, "But the hour comes now when the true worshipers shall worship the Father in spirit and in the truth, for the Father seeks such to worship Him." I was worshiping Him the way Jesus worships Him.

I got up from my bed. I walked around the room thinking about what had just happened. Outside was getting light. I looked through the big glass doors—everything looked the same to me; the world had not changed. But I knew that something was different. I was different. On the other side of my window, it was gloomy and dark, rain was pouring down, and the day was dawning like all the days before. But I was seeing the world in a new way. The world looked beautiful to me.

I was changed, I was new, I was different. It was the first day of my life—a new beginning, a new future, was standing in front of me. I thought about my past and felt so unworthy, so small, and so insignificant. Why had all this happened to me? Then I remembered how much God loves me. I knew what my God was and how He was seeing me. I felt privileged, and I felt honored. I was cleansed, and I was pure.

My past was behind me. I knew that nothing was ever going to separate me from my God. He was the biggest treasure of my life. I was walking into my future, and I was not alone anymore.

And I wondered—What is my new future going to be like?